The Legend

of the Lighter

AD VAN WEERT

The Legend
of the Lighter

TEXT JOOP BROMET

AD & ALICE VAN WEERT

ABBEVILLE PRESS PUBLISHERS
NEW YORK LONDON PARIS

First published in the United States of America in 1995 by Abbeville Press, 488 Madison Avenue, New York, N.Y. 10022.
First published in the Netherlands in 1995 by V+K Publishing, Rembrandtlaan 41, 1412 JN Naarden and the Dutch Lighter Museum Foundation, Eindhoven, the Netherlands.

ISBN 1-55859-854-5

Front cover: A: Consul Druco gasoline and flint wheel table lighter by Köllisch Brothers, Nuremberg, Germany, c. 1938. Brass with chromium plating.
B: Altenpohl & Pilgram GmbH gasoline and flint wheel table lighter, Germany, c. 1935. Brass with chromium plating and mother-of-pearl.
C: Refill tank.

Back cover: Touch-Tip Octette gasoline and flint wheel table lighter by Ronson, Great Britain, c. 1952. Brass and aluminum with chromium plating and enamel. This lighter appears in the logo of the Dutch Lighter Museum Foundation.

· · · · · · · · · · · ·

Frontispiece: Rowenta gasoline and flint wheel table lighter, model F-4507, Germany, c. 1950. Brass with chromium plating and leather binding. Pocket lighter, Germany, c. 1950. Brass with chromium plating and celluloid band.

Title page: Indian pump drill with flywheel, North America, c. 1700s. Ivory Eskimo fire stick with boreholes made from walrus tusk. Wooden Eskimo fire stick. Boris and Maya Rubin, New York.

· · · · · · · · · · · ·

Above: Leaflet for Consul Druco table lighter.

· · · · · · · · · · · ·

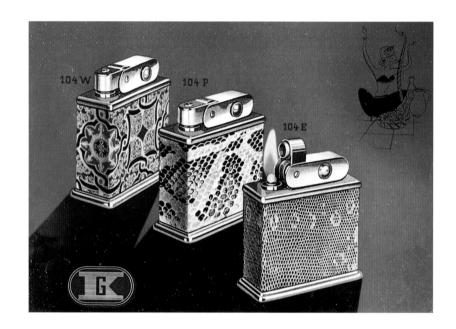

For my dear wife, Alice, who gave her last strength to this book but was unable to witness the results of her labor.

Note: Captions are keyed to the photographs alphabetically from top to bottom and from left to right. All lighters are from the collection of the Dutch Lighter Museum Foundation, Eindhoven, the Netherlands, unless otherwise stated.

Concept
Ad van Weert, Nuenen
Richard Peersmann, Roelofarendsveen

Editor in Chief
Ad van Weert, Nuenen

Coordination
Alice van Weert, Nuenen

Text and Editing
Joop Bromet, Apeldoorn
Ad & Alice van Weert, Nuenen

Designers
Jan Johan ter Poorten and
José K. Vermeulen, Naarden

Translator
Lynn George, Amsterdam

Editor
Alice Gray, New York

Production Editor
Owen Dugan, New York

Photography
Studio Bob van Tienhoven, Weesp

Contents

6   Foreword

9   1 The Birth of the Lighter
A Journey of Daring and Discovery

13   2 Origins
The Harnessing of Fire

23   3 The Age of Invention
Science and Industry Light Up

43   4 Innovation and Progress
A Cavalcade of New Products

101   5 Postwar Revolution
From Gasoline to Gas Lighters

153   6 A New Era Dawns
The Global Market and the Future of the Lighter

186   Donors

187   Bibliography

188   Index

192   Acknowledgments

FOREWORD

Since the dawn of civilization, fire has played a central role in the progress of humankind and the development of both industry and culture. While our cave-dwelling ancestors feared and revered the seemingly magical flames that alighted in the forest, their more advanced progeny learned to control, and eventually to make, fire. Once human beings had established their mastery over fire, they were no longer merely prey to the elements; they could concentrate on tasks such as making tools and weapons and gathering and cultivating food; essentially, they could begin the process of becoming civilized. Forging ahead toward greater and greater sophistication, people of every era have attempted to devise the best means of fire-making – from the primitive tools of the Bronze and Iron Ages to the fire steels of ancient Greece to the tinderboxes of the seventeenth century to today's microelectronic lighters.

As the culmination of humankind's search for an efficient and portable fire-source, the development of the lighter truly reflects the progress of civilization. The history of the lighter is an illuminating chart of our long journey from prehistoric times to the present, and it is this fascinating story that is told in this book.

Although the basic function of the modern lighter recalls the earliest and simplest fire-makers, it is also a marvel of ingenuity and versatile design. And it is this appealing marriage of technique and design – notable in nearly every model that has been produced – that has made the lighter a highly desirable collector's item.

Lighter enthusiasts from all over the world gather regularly at conventions and exhibitions to exchange information and talk endlessly about this wondrous and wonderful object. Until now, however, there has been a great need for a comprehensive book on the lighter, one which in words and pictures delves deeply into the past, present, and future of this alluring and multi-faceted device. The Legend of the Lighter more than fulfills this need: the book recounts the history of the lighter in captivating detail, beginning with the discovery of fire and ending with a provocative look at the future of the lighter industry.

Many of the illustrations have come from the Dutch Lighter Museum Foundation in Eindhoven, the Netherlands, which has one of the world's largest and most complete collections in this field. The Lighter Museum's holdings illustrate every phase of the development of the lighter; they include patent applications and technical drawings penned by manufacturers and designers, as well as advertisements and, of course, exceptional examples of lighters from every period made in every conceivable shape, form, and material.

Leaflet for Consul Druco table lighter.

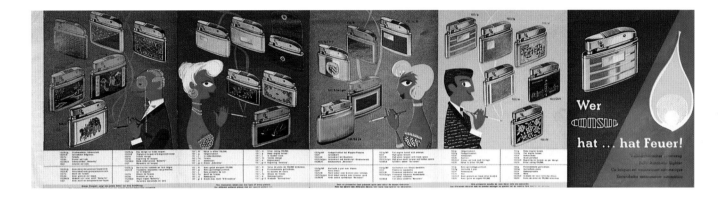

The Legend of the Lighter is the first book to trace the history of the lighter and to place it in its historical and sociological context; the authors have devoted particular attention to the cultural, scientific, and political circumstances that have influenced the development of the lighter. Beautifully illustrated and designed, and written in an engaging style that will appeal to experts, collectors, and novices alike, this book is destined to become a classic reference work that will fascinate both present and future generations. The Legend of the Lighter places the lighter on the pedestal it so rightly deserves.

Richard F. M. Peersmann
Managing director of Pollyflame International / Royal Borsumy Wehry Group, and deputy chairman of the Dutch Lighter Museum Foundation, Eindhoven, the Netherlands.

1

A JOURNEY OF DARING

AND DISCOVERY

The Birth of the Lighter

A: Tinder pistol with candle holder, Great Britain, c. 1700s. Brass, steel, and wood.
B: Tinderbox, Argentina, c. 1700s. Armadillo tail with silver frame.
C: Fire steel with lion, possibly Spain, c. 1700s. Steel and silver. Ad and Annie Jansen, Eindhoven, the Netherlands.

Fire steel with knife, India, c. 1600s/1700s. Steel. Boris and Maya Rubin, New York.

The history of the lighter can be traced back to the harnessing of fire, one of humankind's most essential and powerful discoveries. Since the first sticks and stones were rubbed together in caves across Africa, Asia, and Europe, fire played an unprecedented, pivotal role in the economies and religions of countless early civilizations.

Both a source of warmth and an effective weapon, the development of fire-power allowed primitive communities to survive onslaughts of inclement weather, fresh food shortages, and rampaging enemy tribes. Many early civilizations attributed fire to a divine source, and revered a particular god or mythic hero as the creator or discoverer of this magical – and often destructive – force. According to Greek mythology, the daring giant Prometheus filched fire from the gods on Mount Olympus for the benefit of the mortals below. Among other ancient peoples, the use of fire was restricted to the elite of the tribe, to the magicians or "witch-doctors" who were believed to be endowed with the ability to ignite and tame the divine flames. Across the globe, fire played a central role in marriage and burial rituals: at primitive weddings in southern Africa, the lighting of a fire from two flames was thought to symbolize the unity of the participating tribes; the ancient Indian practice of cremating the dead was believed to purify both body and soul for the journey into the great beyond.

Eventually, fire moved into the realm of science; early philosophers in China, India, and Greece named fire as one of the four basic elements, along with earth, air, and water. In Enlightenment-era Europe, the study of fire remained paramount among eighteenth-century scientists, who discovered that fire, far from being divine, was but one form of heat or "energy," the true life-source for industrialized nations.

Even in our own technology-crazed age, however, fire has retained some of its mysterious and awesome power. We still fear the destructive nature of a fire uncontained; we are still drawn to the unifying warmth of a quietly tended fire at home or in the wilderness. Like our ancestors, we gather by the fireside to eat, to talk, and often, to light a pipe, cigar, or cigarette. Indeed, even the single flame brought forth on a street corner to light a cigarette for an acquaintance or a friend can create a cloak of human warmth and togetherness. Almost as soon as man had harnessed fire for domestic

purposes, the search for a portable, manual fire-source began. From primitive fire pots and bows to seventeenth-century tinderboxes, through the hand-held fire pistons and fusee lighters of the industrial age, to the electric, battery-operated, gasoline-fueled, or butane gas devices of the twentieth century, the development of the lighter has reflected technological advances and cultural trends worldwide. A flaming fire bow, a rough-hewn tinderbox, or a jewel-encrusted lighter shaped like an animal, a globe, or a rifle, tells a rich visual tale about its maker, its user, and the world in which it was created. Today, a portable fire-source is no longer a prized possession or a status symbol; the most common lighter is the disposable sort, often emblazoned with an image or logo from a popular tourist spot. But the simple looks of the common lighter belie its fascinating history – a history filled with illuminating insights into our timeless quest for technological, economic, and cultural achievement.

Ives wheel tinderbox, Bristol, England, c. 1850. Steel with steel plating. Boris and Maya Rubin. This hand-held tinderbox produced a flame when the fire steel was pressed against the wheel and a cord on its side quickly unrolled. The resulting shower of sparks lit the tinder, which was then used to light the accompanying matches.

A: Table tinderbox with sconce, Great Britain, c. 1700s. Brass. Ad and Annie Jansen.
B: Fire steel, c. 1800. Steel.

2

Origins

The Spedding mill, c. 1750. Invented by Carlisle Spedding, who operated the Whitehaven coal mine in England, the Spedding mill is considered the first safety miner's lamp. In earlier days, miners used phosphorescent, rotted fish or a glass jar filled with fireflies for lighting purposes. At the time, people believed that mine gases would only explode in the presence of a flame; the Spedding lamp, therefore, was considered relatively safe because it produced only sparks. When the handle was turned, a steel wheel rapidly rotated, and an adjustable spring pressed the fire steel against this spinning wheel, creating a shower of sparks that fell into the tinderbox. The sparks turned from white to dark red when gas was present in a mine. Spedding's lamp, however, was not as reliable or safe as it first appeared to be: just a few years after completing his invention, Spedding himself died in a mine explosion caused by one of his lamps.

A: Tinderbox, the Netherlands, 1779. Wood, mother-of-pearl, and brass. Ad and Annie Jansen.
B: Tinderbox, numbered 10297, with an illustration of a train and ships, Great Britain, c. 1850. Brass. The box contains the original tinder and flint.

A: Fire steel with an illustration of two swans, Spain, c. 1700s. Steel. B: Oval fire steel, Great Britain, c. 1700s. Steel. Ad and Annie Jansen.

....

Before the invention of the fire pots and drills that preceded the first tinder pistol lighter, heat as we know it was an alien concept to the Earth's human inhabitants. For these largely nomadic tribes, the hides of freshly slaughtered animals were the most readily available source of warmth; fires, when they appeared, were a sign of uncontrollable, perhaps divine, forces at work in a world filled with innumerable, unfathomable mysteries.

Two chuck-mucks, China, c. 1850: one decorated with Chinese symbols that contains a hook, one with a key shaped like fish.

Magnifying glass tinderbox, Great Britain, c. 1700s. Copper and wood. Boris and Maya Rubin.
....

Lightning probably first brought the nomads in contact with fire; we can imagine their surprise – and fear – as they watched these "flashes of fire" stream down from the sky and ignite a tree, or an entire forest. Over the years, people undoubtedly became familiar with the mystery of lightning, though they had yet to solve the riddle of its origin and purpose; everything associated with fire was a powerful phenomenon to which they attributed mythical properties. "Who is the Great Magician who can change a lush meadow into a raging sea of flames?" they must have wondered; "What can we do to appease him?" There were no means, back then, by which to control a fire. Three to five million years ago, our ancestors must have simply stood by and watched as the forest blazed.

There came a time, however, when people realized that fire might not only be seen as a foe, but also as a friend. It occurred to them that fire might be a positive resource: a congenial source of heat, or a griddle for roasting meat, so that it didn't have to be eaten raw. Anthropologists have also discovered that many prehistoric cultures understood the practical uses of periodically burning sections of the forest. Some Asian and African tribes, for example, developed the means for starting forest fires in areas they had chosen for

planting. It was on this land, cleared by burning, that they practiced the earliest known forms of cultivation.

Even as these early communities evolved into fledgling civilizations and began to grasp the practical uses of fire, they continued to attribute a divine significance to the making or appearance of fire, often worshipping a particular god or mythic hero as its source. As we know, the early Greeks credited Prometheus (his name literally means "one who thinks in advance") with bringing fire hidden in a reed down from Mount Olympus to Earth, and fire gods and fire priests appear in the religion and folklore of most other early civilizations. Those who made or protected fire were often considered holy or inviolable, and they and their duties were enveloped in ritual and taboo. The Vestal Virgins, who provided fire for ancient Rome, symbolized religious and political unity. The importance of their position – and of the guarding of the sacred fire – was evident in their requisite shunning of all earthly attachments; they could not fall in love or marry during their years of service, and hence took a vow of chastity before assuming their duties. The Virgin whose flesh was too weak to maintain her promise was sentenced to death. Fire has also had special significance in those religions that

have prevailed into the twentieth century. In Islamic, Jewish, and Christian holy texts, fire appears frequently as a symbol for a holy offering or a sign of prophecy. According to the Bible, fire is also the chief component of the misery in the after-life that is promised to sinners.

Fire pots and fire horns

Our ancestors pursued the magic of fire for practical, as well as divine, purposes, and even before anyone realized that fire could be produced by rubbing sticks or stones together, they set out to devise a way to preserve the valuable flames they found glowing in the wilderness. Usually, the joy of having captured fire from nature was short-lived, as rain often extinguished the burning twigs, or the tribe had to relocate and was unable to carry or sustain their fire en route. A solution was eventually found: to save fire, dry materials, such as leaves, were stuffed into pots made of stone or bamboo or into animal horns, and smoldering twigs were wedged in between the leaves. The whole was then tightly compressed and tiny holes were made in the pot for ventilation. When the fire went out, the container was swung around, thus creating the air flow needed to rekindle the flames. Fire pots provided the best means of conserving and transporting fire for these nomadic people, who were still unable to start a fire at will.

Fire drills and bows

Finally, perhaps on a cold and wintry day in the sparsely populated wilderness, a tribe member must have noticed that by rubbing two twigs together, a remarkable thing happens: the wood begins to smolder. That very evening, he sits with the rest of the tribe around what will hopefully become a campfire, displaying what he has learned. Silently, they rub the wood

Walnut netsuke flintlock mechanism with tinder and fire steel, Japan, c. 1750. Steel and brass.

A: Pocket tinder pistol, Great Britain, c. 1700s. Steel. Ad and Annie Jansen.
B: Tinder pistol, the Netherlands, c. 1750. Steel and wood.

....

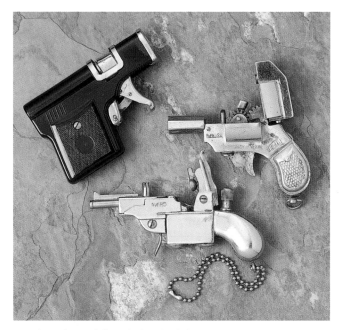

A: Puck gasoline and flint wheel pocket lighter, Germany, c. 1940. Bakelite and brass with chromium plating. B: Dandy gasoline and flint wheel pocket lighter, possibly Austria, c. 1920. Marked "ME & JB, US patent." Brass with chromium plating. C: Unmarked. Stamped "China" (written backwards). China, c. 1940. Brass, chromium plated.

A: Streamline 6800 gasoline and flint wheel pocket lighter by Imco, Austria, c. 1960. Bakelite with beaten and lacquered chromium-plated steel. This is an Imco prototype that incorporates the Streamline 6800 lighter into a pistol design. This particular lighter never went into production, although the butt of the pistol contains an information label from the design department of Imco. B: Gasoline and flint wheel pocket lighter, Germany, c. 1960. Aluminum with lacquered and chromium plated steel. C: Beretta gasoline and flint wheel pocket lighter by Modern, Japan, c. 1975. Lacquered metal alloy with plastic shields.

••••••••••••

16
••••••••

A: Silver Match gas and flint wheel table lighter, France, c. 1965. Metal alloy with wooden stand. B: Windsor gasoline and flint wheel table lighter, Colt model 5206, Japan, c. 1971. Gilded brass with lacquered metal alloy. C: Gasoline and flint wheel table lighter, Japan. Lacquered metal alloy with gilded brass.

••••••••••••

together, and in no time at all, they have created enough heat for a fire. Quickly, they throw straw or dried wood and blow softly until ignition takes place.

Meanwhile, another tribe thousands of miles away is making tools, such as arrowheads and celts, from pyrite stones. As they knock the stones together, sparks begin to alight on the dry grass underneath. As soon as man realized he could actually make his own fire – he was not dependent on the whims of nature or the gods to send flames periodically shooting into the forest – he began to experiment with various methods and materials. The Polynesians discovered that a fire could be produced more rapidly if two different types of wood (a hard wood and a soft wood, for example) were rubbed together. To encourage friction, sand was sometimes scattered between the two pieces of wood. In the areas now known as Indonesia and the Philippines, bamboo and stone were the most popular fire-making instruments, while Eskimos preferred using walrus teeth.

Soon, more efficient, less exhausting, ways came into use. The early fire drill consisted of a stick with a flywheel and a primitive rotating device that was pressed onto a plank of wood until it smoldered. The smoldering wood was then used to set other dry wood or straw ablaze. Firesticks, fire saws, and fire ploughs were also developed according to this basic model.

The Iron Age (circa 1000 BC) had a profound effect on early fire-making. With the discovery of iron, it became possible to knock sparks out of pieces of flint using an iron pyrite "fire steel." The sparks, made of minuscule splinters of burning iron, fell onto dry material, or tinder, and smoldered; oxygen was supplied by blowing onto the pile and a blazing fire was created. This method was later adapted with great success by blacksmiths, who, until relatively recently, fanned their fires with bellows that blew great gusts of air into the flames.

According to historical studies and excavations, the ancient Greeks and Romans used fire steels extensively. These were often crafted in the shape of a ram's head: the iron was thought to symbolize strength, the flame purity, and the ram power. The most famous image ever emblazoned on a fire steel was made from the links of a golden chain on which the symbol of the Order of the Golden Fleece was hung. This

medieval-era Christian organization took its name from the heroic mythical quest of the Greek Argonaut sailors, who originally captured the golden fleece. The owner of a fire steel emblazoned with this symbol was thought to be protected by the power of his belief, and would be able to fight with the strength of iron for Christendom. The ram remained a common image on fire steels, and family coats of arms were also frequently added. In some parts of the world, a fire steel was the only way to make fire for centuries. In fact, this basic method of knocking iron against flint was only really improved upon in the eighteenth century, when the flowering of physics and chemistry led to spectacular new advances in fire-making.

Tinder mushrooms

The discovery that a spark on dry wood creates a fire was quickly followed by the search for supplies of dry fuel. Arab nomads often used camel dung in the desert, but Europeans had no such readily available and usable source. Due to frequent rainfall, wooden baskets and grass were often too damp to ignite quickly, so Europeans looking for fuel had to create an alternative in the form of tinder. Tinder is a generic term for fuel made from anything from scorched linen or cotton to sawdust and organic substances. The most famous

European tinder was discovered near the German cities of Ulm and Neustadt: it was a brown-gray mushroom, Fomes fomentarius, which came to be known as the tinder mushroom. It is hoof-shaped, sometimes reaching a half-meter in width, and after processing, is suitable for a variety of purposes. In medicine, the mushroom was used as a styptic agent to stop bleeding (hence its second name, Fungus chirurgorum); it was even used to make women's hats.

The tinder mushroom proved to be an extremely effective substance for lighting fires. During summer, the mushrooms were gathered from beech, oak, or birch trees. Their tough exteriors were removed and they were treated with lye and then tapped with a wooden tool to make them fibrous and more flammable. Later, saltpeter (potassium nitrate or sodium nitrate) and calcium chloride were applied to increase their combustibility. A lucrative trade in mushroom tinder developed in around these two cities by the end of the seventeenth century. In fact, Neustadt eventually became known as Schwamm ("Mushroom")-Neustadt. In 1840, local industries in these areas began producing matches and the tinder mushroom trade dwindled, although a few people continued to look for the flammable mushrooms into the early twentieth century.

A: Corona gasoline and flint wheel pocket lighter, model 45, Japan, c. 1960. Lacquered metal alloy, and brass with chromium plating; plastic shields. B: Helenix gasoline and flint wheel pocket lighter, Japan. c.1975. Brass with chromium plating and plastic shields.

A: Gas with piezo ignition pocket lighter, model FC 555 Gun V, Taiwan, patented 1990. Lacquered plastic with metal shields. B: K.K. Apollo gasoline and flint wheel table lighter, c. 1948. C: Gasoline and flint wheel table lighter, Japan c. 1948. Marked "Made in occupied Japan." Brass with chromium plating and plastic shields.

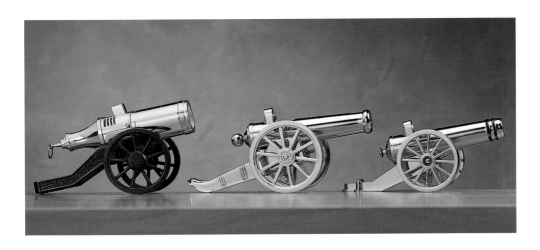

A: *Gasoline and flint wheel table lighter, Japan, c. 1965. Gilded brass with lacquered metal alloy.*
B: *A.T.C. gasoline and flint wheel table lighter, Japan, c. 1965. Metal alloy and brass with chromium plating.*
C: *Gasoline and flint wheel table lighter, Japan. c. 1964. Metal alloy with lacquer and chromium plating.*

Negbaur gasoline and flint wheel table lighter, United States, c. 1945. Metal alloy with patina.

19

Tinderboxes

Around 1600, boxes, tins, and pouches in which flint, fire steel, and tinder could be stored began to appear. Tinderboxes were made in a variety of sizes, ranging from very large ones intended for display to smaller, pocket-sized models. Leather pouches for storing tinder were often attached to clothing with a buckle or belt. Until the late nineteenth century, the tinderbox was a trusty companion to people from all walks of life; you could tell a person's social standing from the value of his tinderbox. Lumberjacks, shepherds, and soldiers carried simpler tinderboxes than the more prosperous members of the middle and upper classes, who had theirs made in expensive materials such as brass, silver, or ivory. The owner's initials, and preferably the family coat of arms, were also engraved on the box. Valuable tinderboxes might also be made from precious metals and rare, exotic, materials, such as armadillo tails from South America and crocodile teeth from India.

The round English tinderboxes made during the late eighteenth century are particularly interesting. In these, the flint and steel have been replaced by a reflective glass that caught the sun's rays and thereby ignited the tinder. These tinderboxes were produced in extremely limited editions, which is indicative both of their cost and of the British climate, where strong, natural sunlight is often scarce. These tinderboxes are highly prized by collectors today.

The wheel tinderbox also dates from the eighteenth century. Similar to a spinning top, the wheel is spun with a rope along the flints until sparks fly onto the tinder, lighting the fire. The increasing mechanization of tinderboxes such as these points toward the beginning of the industrial revolution.

Tinderboxes were quickly adapted for domestic use, although those used at the hearth were far simpler in both design and materials than those displayed in the drawing room or on the street. Often, a domestic tinderbox consisted of no more than a wooden or thin metal barrel with a lid, a handle, and sometimes a socket, so that it could also be used as a candlestick. During the late eighteenth century, beautifully decorated brass tinderboxes began to appear in the kitchens of the well-to-do; this material is less sensitive to oxidization than iron and can withstand constant changes in temperature during cooking. For the most part, these were produced chiefly in England and the Netherlands and exported to other countries.

Chuck-mucks

The Asian equivalent of the tinderbox is the chuck-muck, which was made from a leather pouch with a sewn-in fire steel and space for the flint and tinder. The name is derived from the Old English words for steel and stone and it operated according to the same method as the European tinderbox, with one important difference: in Europe, a separate fire steel was often used, attached by a chain to the tinderbox. All the components of the chuck-muck, on the other hand, were kept in one pouch. The chuck-muck was especially popular in Tibet, Burma, Nepal, and Afghanistan, and was often exquisitely decorated; as with the tinderbox, the simplicity or elaborateness of the design depended upon the owner's social standing. Chuck-mucks and tinderboxes can be considered the forebears of the modern lighter, though they did not yet include a truly efficient lighting device. This problem was partially solved by the proliferation of sulfur matches during

the nineteenth century; these were easy to light with the glowing embers of the tinder, much like the modern matches we use today.

Tinder pistols

The earliest lighter, known as the tinder pistol, vastly improved upon the tinderbox and chuck-muck. It was invented during the mid-seventeenth century, shortly after the first pistols were made. Developed some three hundred years after the discovery of gunpowder by a fourteenth-century German monk named Berthold Schwarz, these first pistols functioned in a relatively straightforward manner: powder was packed into the barrel followed by a lead ball and the powder ignited through a small hole by the sparks produced by a flint held in the jaws of the cock hitting a flat steel plate discharging the ball. This device gave gunsmiths the idea of recycling broken pistols by replacing the barrel with a container in which tinder could be stored. Mixed with a little gunpowder, this produced a fantastic effect – a burst of flame. Because they were the first mechanical device for making fire, they are considered by historians and collectors the earliest lighters. Demand for tinder pistols grew rapidly. Some were designed for display on a table at home with an accompanying candleholder, clock, or inkwell; for the more military-minded, others were made to be worn on the body; and many were handsomely engraved with the owner's name or initials. The legacy of the tinder pistol continues today, as lighters shaped like guns are still produced.

Japanese netsukes

Among Asian cultures, the Japanese were especially eager to develop a portable igniting device, although their designs had to account for some factors that were unknown to Westerners. Japanese clothing did not lend itself to carrying anything on one's person; kimonos might be practical and colorful, but they did have the disadvantage of lacking pockets. If one wished to carry a purse, notepad, tobacco, etc., a bag attached to a netsuke, or toggle, which hung from the waist, was needed. Often made from walnut wood, the netsuke had holes through which a cord was drawn; it was a decorative substitute for the handbag or trouser pocket. An entire culture evolved around the netsuke; they were carved in ivory and in lacquered wood and painted by artists with motifs ranging from history, folklore, and mythology, to flora and fauna, legends, and proverbs. Many netsukes also functioned as telescopic brushes, ink pads, or paper cutters. As smoking in Japan became markedly more widespread during the second half of the eighteenth century, a special culture developed around the making of netsukes for smokers. A tremendous variety of designs evolved, including some that were made as both a bag for tobacco and an étui, or decorative case. The European tinder pistol was also imaginatively translated, in miniature, into a netsuke. Eventually, netsukes became virtually synonymous with portable tobacco containers and lighters.

Optical lighters

The Chinese were particularly ingenious in their development and application of the large-scale, optical lighter, which was inspired by an ancient tradition popular among many early communities of using a glass lens or reflective mirror to direct the sun's rays onto a large, centrally located object and thereby ignite a fire. Before the proliferation of mechanical clocks, many large village parks in China had a cannon on which a lens was attached pointing at the barrel. When the sun was high in the sky, it shone through the lens, but only at noon was the ideal position reached that caused the gunpowder in the cannon to explode. Then, everyone far and wide knew that it was midday, and early the next morning a fresh supply of gunpowder would be delivered to the site.

Parabolic mirrors and lenses were also used by the early Tibetans and Incans; the sun-priests who led their communities derived their authority and power from their ability to create fire by using these curved, reflective instruments to direct the sun's rays. The ancient Greeks were also apparently familiar with optical methods of fire-making. Aristophanes's comedy The Clouds mentions a glass that conducts energy from the sun, and the Thracian singer Orpheus sang about a fire being lit through a lens that acts as a magnifying glass for the sun's rays.

Today, there is only one occasion on which a fire is purposely ignited this way: on the eve of the Olympic Games. The first marathon runner, who travels by foot to the host city, must light his or her torch in Greece using the energy of the sun. Lighters that include parabolic mirrors or lenses are still produced, though today they are generally made from plastic and are largely regarded as curios. They remain popular, however, among mountain climbers, and they function much the same way they did hundreds of years ago; when everything is wet after a rain shower, all these lighters need to produce a healthy flame is a ray of sunlight.

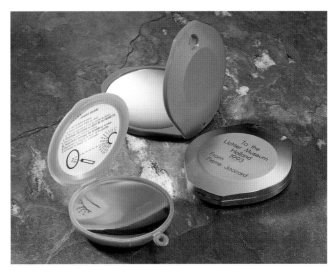

A: Ray-star solar pocket lighter, Switzerland, c. 1984. Plastic. A brass prototype of this model is in the collection of the Dutch Lighter Museum. B: Ray-star solar pocket lighter, Switzerland, c. 1984. C: Silver Match solar pocket lighter, France, c. 1965. Plastic.
A: Super Ra magnifying glass pocket lighter, Switzerland, c. 1978. Plastic. B: Solar Match magnifying glass pocket lighter, Austria, c. 1985. Plastic.

SOLAR-MATCH

SUN
SOLEIL

Caution! To avoid risk of accidental fires, do not leave your Solar-Match in the sun. Keep out of reach of children.

3

SCIENCE AND INDUSTRY

LIGHT UP

The Age of Invention

Döbereiner lamp by J. Cassel, Vienna, c. 1835. Glass, brass, and wood. Ad and Annie Jansen.

Fire pump encased in a walking stick, France, patented 1892. Bamboo and brass with chromium plating. Boris and Maya Rubin. When the piston, which held a piece of tinder on its underside, was vigorously forced into the cylinder inside the walking stick, enough heat was generated to ignite the tinder. A compartment for spare tinder is also on the underside of the walking stick.

....

The period known as the industrial revolution, which roughly spans the mid-eighteenth to mid-nineteenth centuries, brought swift and sweeping changes to Europe. Every industry underwent a radical transformation, including the production of fire-making devices. By the early twentieth century, the tinderbox had had its day; consumers wanted other, more expedient and cheaper, alternatives.

Johann Wolfgang Döbereiner discovered the catalytic system that became the basis for the Döbereiner lamp on August 23, 1823. According to Döbereiner's findings, the action of zinc on sulfuric acid produces hydrogen gas. In the Döbereiner lamp, this hydrogen gas bubble caused the sulfuric acid to sink until it was no longer in contact with the zinc and the reaction ceased. The gas remained pressurized in a container; when the small tap on the top of the lighter was opened, the hydrogen gas sprayed onto platinum wool, and this catalytic reaction produced a flame. Using a wooden splinter, the flame could be used to light a cigarette. After the initial ignition, pressure in the gas container decreased sufficiently for the acid to rise again and the process could be repeated. When both handles on the lighter were pressed down, the gasoline tank shifted between the tap and the platinum wool, igniting the fusee. Next to this Döbereiner lamp is a bottle of alcohol; its cork could be used to transport a flame in place of a wooden splinter.

•••••••••••

A: Match holder with fusee by Christine Nilsson, France, c. 1870. Gilded brass. *Ad and Annie Jansen.* An inscription on the inside of the box indicates that the matches were imported by "L. G.," Louis Germot, an importer of matches in Paris. B: Match holder with fusee, Great Britain, c. 1880. Brass. C: Match holder with fusee, Germany, c. 1865. Brass with chromium plating. The fusee was often used in place of matches, which were scarce during the late nineteenth century. Fusees were also used to light cannons during *World War I.*

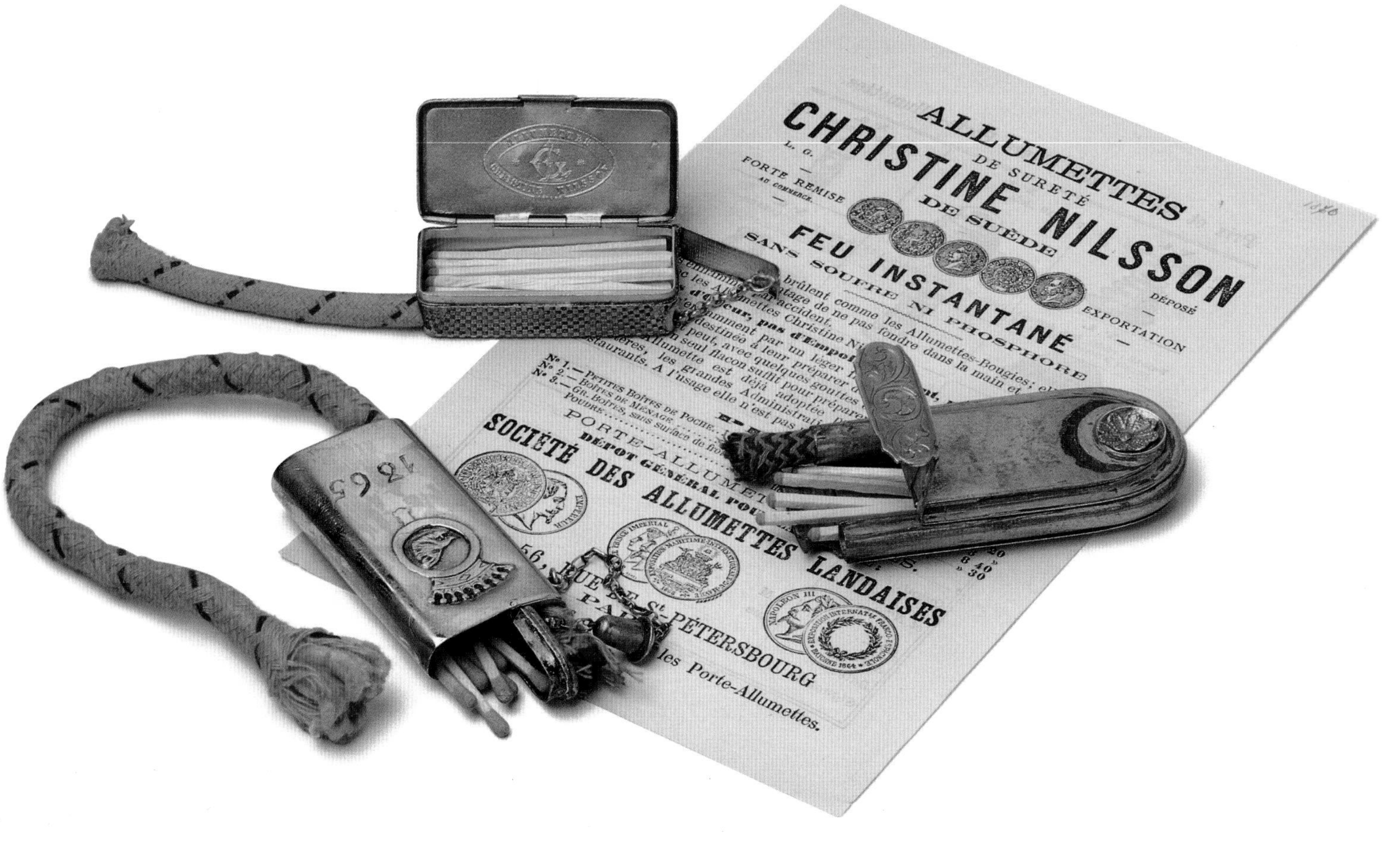

•••••••••••

25

A: Fire steel with fusee, Germany, c. 1850. Steel and brass with chromium plating.
B: Gorin fire steel, France, c. 1890. Marked "A. G. Déposé." Steel and brass with chromium plating.
C: Fire steel with fusee, the Netherlands, c. 1810. Steel and silver. *Ad and Annie Jansen.*

A: Match holder with fusee, Great Britain, c. 1850. Gilded brass and leather.
B: Match holder with fusee, possibly Spain, c. 1850. Steel and gold leaf. This extremely distinctive model, which opens mechanically when the front and back of the holder are pressed at the same time, has overlays of two different colors of gold.
C: Match holder with fusee, Great Britain, c. 1880. Silver.

....

Luminus gasoline table lighter with an electro-chemical filament, France, c. 1880. Glass and brass with chromium plating.

....

The blue bottle, which is filled with a potassium bichromate-based liquid, contains two carbon electrodes. By pressing a button, a zinc electrode is brought into contact with the liquid and electricity is produced. The green bottle, filled with gasoline, contains two fusees. The top opens when a button is pressed, causing the platinum coil next to the smaller fusee to glow. As the small fusee burns, it lights the larger fusee outside the top. When the top is closed again, no more electricity is produced.

....

ELIAS BERNARD KOOPMAN in NEW-YORK (V. St. A.).

Schlagfeuerzeug mit selbstthätiger Zündung.

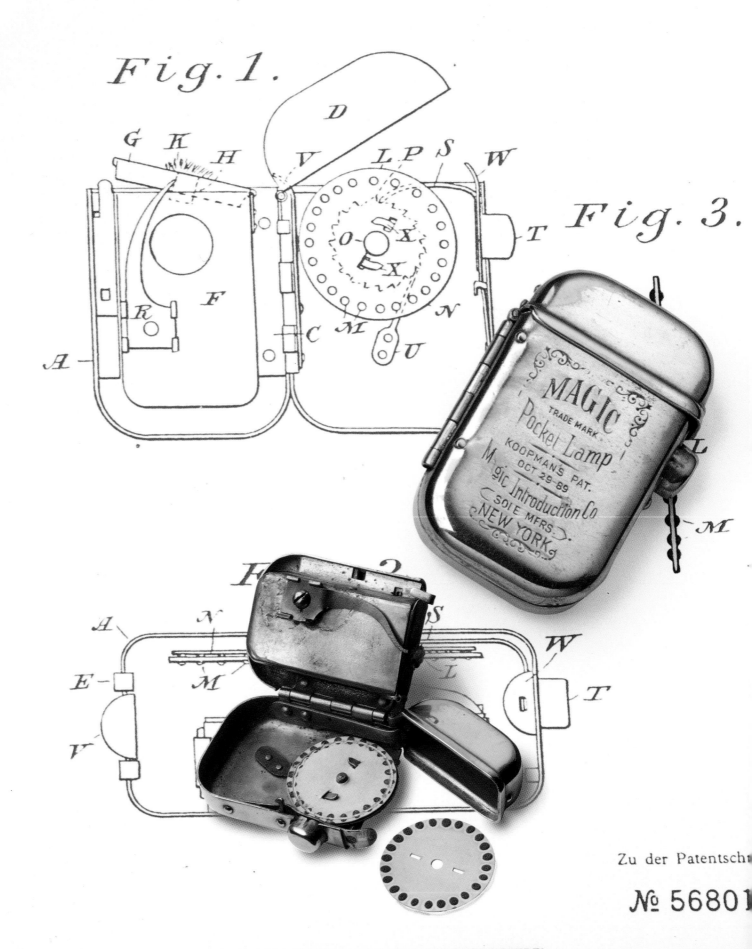

Fig. 1.

Fig. 2.

Fig. 3.

PHOTOGR. DRUCK DER REICHSDRUCKEREI.

Zu der Patentsch

Scientists began searching for the perfect ingredients for an efficient lighter, and in Sweden, inventors came up with the safety match. Demand for these innovations grew rapidly, especially at the end of the Crimean War (1854–56), when cigarette smoking gained widespread popularity in Europe.

Prior to the eighteenth century, chemistry was a fledgling science, though a few scientists and other prominent thinkers were already challenging the theory of the four basic elements, particularly the notion that fire was one of these. The English metaphysical poet John Donne (1572–1631) predicted the debunking of this theory in his An Anatomy of the World (1611), and was hence dubbed "the Copernicus of poetry." It was not until a century and a half later, however, that Donne was proven right and fire was shown to be but one manifestation of heat, which could be produced through a chemical reaction. In 1777, a Frenchman named Antoine Laurent Lavoisier conducted a series of experiments and discovered a link between oxygen and combustion that replaced the concept of fire as an independent entity with the modern notions of heat and energy. Lavoisier's findings did not delineate the precise nature of heat – this would come much later – but they did establish the creation of heat through combustion. Today, Lavoisier is honored as the father of modern chemistry.

Döbereiners

Lavoisier's discovery of combustion had a direct and decisive effect on the development of fire-making devices: the death knell was sounded for the fire steel and tinderbox. More and more scientists began devoting their energies to finding better, quicker ways to turn spark to flame. In 1780, a Swiss chemist

A: Koopman's Magic Pocket Lamp by Magic Introduction Co., United States, c. 1889. Brass with chromium plating. This patented design is a gasoline pocket lighter with an exploding cap disc and scriber.
B: Koopman's Magic Pocket Lamp, opened to show the scratcher above the fuel tank. In the foreground is a spare cap disc.

A: Fulmen Pinel gasoline pocket lighter with exploding cap tape and hammer, Belgium, c. 1890. Brass with chromium plating. This model includes an automatic hammer system.
B: Stockwell fusee pocket lighter with exploding cap tape and hammer, United States, c. 1865. Brass with chromium plating.
C: Fusee pocket lighter with exploding cap tape and hammer, United States, c. 1877. Brass with chromium plating.

· · · · · · · · · · ·

named Johannes Fürstenberger came up with a device for igniting hydrogen gas (created through the action of sulfuric acid on zinc) using electric sparks.

Almost fifty years later, in 1823, the renowned German chemist Johann Wolfgang Döbereiner perfected this principle and produced a table lighter suitable for domestic use. The Döbereiner lighter created its own hydrogen gas through the action of sulfuric acid on zinc; a platinum sponge then acted as a catalyst for the gas, instantly producing a flame. Döbereiner, a chemistry professor in Jena, and a friend and advisor to Goethe, counted other significant discoveries among his accomplishments, including the Law of the Triads, which states that the atomic weight of the second of three elements with similar properties is the average of the others. This finding eventually led to the establishment of the periodic table for the classification of elements.

The Döbereiner gas table lighter, aptly named for its inventor, was a great success and was rapidly put into production. Early versions were made of glass, so that the entire chemical process could be carefully studied. Later, when this device had proven its worth throughout Europe, Döbereiners were also made from other materials. These were often exquisitely painted, and they became a standard feature of every gentleman's den. It is estimated that some 20,000 Döbereiners were made since their introduction in 1823 – a large number considering that only the wealthy could afford them.

A: Fusee pocket lighter with separate percussion caps and hammer, United States, c. 1880. Brass. Boris and Maya Rubin.
B: Gasoline pocket lighter with separate percussion caps and hammer, United States, c. 1885. Brass. Boris and Maya Rubin. In both of these lighters, a small hammer was used to explode the caps so that the fusee either glowed or burned. The fusee had to approach the point of explosion in order to ignite.

A: Köhlers gasoline pocket lighter with exploding cap and tape, Germany, c. 1885. Brass. A lever on the underside of the lighter transported the tape; the hammer hit the caps, which then ignited the fusee.
B: Gasoline pocket lighter with exploding cap tape and hammer, possibly Köhlers, Germany, c. 1890. Brass with chromium plating.

············

Most have now disappeared, in part because they were not particularly safe; sometimes the hydrogen gas made the lighter explode. Perhaps because of the risky shortcomings of his invention, Döbereiner eventually lost interest in improving his design. Fortunately, other, simpler devices were being developed around the same time that were blessed with a longer life span.

Fire piston lighters

In fact, an alternative to the Döbereiner had already existed since the turn of the century. An early fire piston lighter was developed in 1770 by two Parisian brothers, Louis Joseph and François Dumontier. Their invention was based on the discovery that compressed gas releases enough heat for the combustion required to create a smolder, and it worked much like a cycle pump. A piston was forced vigorously down a cylinder and the resulting air compression produced heat that lit the tinder located at the tip of the piston. In 1803, this system was improved upon by the work of a fellow-Frenchman, Joseph Mollet; five years later, the fire piston

Gasoline table lighter with exploding cap tape, hammer, and built-in cigar cutter, Great Britain, c. 1880. Brass and bronze. Boris and Maya Rubin.

The same lighter, opened to reveal two levers in the shape of snakes. When pressed together, the levers transported the tape and the hammer hit the powder. At the same time, a knife passed along a hole in the middle of the lighter to cut off the tip of a cigar; the tip then dropped into a small, removable box.

••••••••••••

Reliable gasoline lighter with exploding cap tape and scriber by Pocketlamp, Philadelphia, patented October 28, 1890. Brass with chromium plating. The action of a rotating wheel transported the tape and exploded the caps.

A: Magic Wax phosphorus paraffin tape pocket lighter with scriber by Magic Introduction Company, United States, c. 1891. Marked "WAX LIGHTER, US patent 2 June 1891/pat. Germany 25 May 1890." Boris and Maya Rubin. Brass with chromium plating.

·············

lighter was introduced to the market in Berlin. These lighters were usually made from fifteen- to twenty-centimeter-long pipes of glass, wood, or metal. Some opened on the underside, where the fuel was stored, so that the flame could be exposed. Outside of Europe, this invention was not new; in southeast Asia, people were already using bamboo fire pistons based on the same principle. In fact, it is entirely possible that the Asian version of the fire piston lighter was imported to France and was simply given a European "interpretation."

Fusee lighters

A number of lighters made during the nineteenth century consisted of a fire steel and flint (usually a piece of pyrite), along with a cotton fusee (a combination of an archaic wick or piece of cord and lighter fuel), which served the same purpose the tinder mushroom did in the earlier tinderbox. Cotton fusees had been in use since the fifteenth century, when they were used to ignite weapons, such as muskets, but it was only several hundred years later that they were employed in making lighters. Around 1880, the first version of the fusee lighter appeared in which the outdated, manual fire steel of stone or iron was replaced by a system of cogs and gears, which transformed the slow turning action of the fire steel into the speedier rotation of a steel wheel. The fusee was pushed up out of a metal tube and held against the resulting fire of sparks until it smoldered. In later versions, the fusee was immersed in gasoline, so that it burned rather than smoldered. Both the flame and the heat were completely extinguished when the wick was dropped back into the casing and covered by a cap. Fusee lighters are still in use, both for practical and sentimental reasons. They are particularly popular at sea, for even when a storm hits, the fusee's glow is so intense that a cigarette or pipe can easily be lit on deck. In Spain, fusee, or cord, lighters are also sold today as souvenirs.

Magic pocket lamps

Around 1889, a new type of lighter employing the fusee came on the market that became extremely popular. Known as the "magic pocket lamp," it used percussion caps similar to those used today for firing toy pistols. The caps were placed on a round cardboard disc; by pressing a button, the lid opened and a transport lever rotated the disc forward; a scriber struck the disc, exploding the powder and setting the gasoline-drenched fusee alight. This method was also used to light gas lamps and street lights. As with the cap pistol, the magic pocket lamp's discs were sold separately from the lamp itself.

The function of the magic pocket lamp is also similar to the phosphorus tape method that was often used to light miner's lamps. This consisted of a paraffin-soaked taped dotted with phosphorus pellets. The pellets were ignited one by one so that the tape would continue burning for a considerable period of time.

 In these wax lighters, the action of a lever moving up and down transported both the paraffin wax tape and the phosphorus pellets; the tape was ignited by a metal strip with teeth. This system was also used for lighting miner's lamps, although a less volatile fuel, such as oil or kerosene was used. Gasoline and other more flammable fuels were readily ignited by the brief explosion of the percussion caps in wax lighters. Caps or pellets could be inserted separately or embedded in a tape or disc, and a scriber was used for the paraffin tape, while either a scriber or a hammer could be used to explode the percussion caps.

·············

Bewick & / Alese Bewick table lighter and stearin candle with phosphorus cap and scriber, Great Britain, c. 1870. Brass with patina. When pressed together, the two levers on this lighter rotated a disc with candles. On each side of the candle is a phosphorus pellet, which scratched a metal point as it rotated, thereby igniting and subsequently lighting the candle.

Miner's lamp with phosphorus paraffin tape and scriber, Germany, c. 1880. Brass and steel.

·············

A: Fusee and emery flint pocket lighter, Great Britain,
c. 1885. Brass with chromium plating.
B: Matchless pyrite flint pocket lighter, United States,
c. 1897. Marked "The Matchless cigar lighter, pat.
27 April 1897, USA." Brass with chromium plating.
A rapidly rotating metal disc caused the pyrite to press
against the disc; the resulting shower of sparks lit the
fusee. The Ives wheel tinderbox operated much the same
way.

············

Emery stone and other late nineteenth-century lighters

As the nineteenth century drew to a close, lighters began to
increasingly resemble those we are familiar with today. Emery
stone, a hard mineral often used as a polishing and grinding
agent, was adapted for use as flint, along with the traditional
pyrite. In 1878, a Frenchman named Joseph Vaudaine patented
a lighter using emery stone that foreshadowed our modern
ones. It consisted of a small emery wheel that rubbed against a
piece of metal, producing a profuse shower of sparks, which in
turn ignited the fusee.

A decade or so later, electric wall lighters were introduced
for domestic use, along with those that ran on batteries. The
lighter had now become an everyday object, and was poised
– along with a thousand and one other inventions – to make the
great leap into the industrialized landscape of the twentieth
century.

The emery flint wheel mechanism was based on a system of cogs and gears. The quick movement of a lever or turning of a ring rotated the wheel along metal plates, and the resulting shower of sparks ignited the fusee. Joseph Vaudaine's 1881 model also included a built-in match holder as a guarantee that a flame could be produced — an added bonus that was later incorporated into the first ferro-cerium flint wheel lighters.

••••••••••••

Joseph Vaudaine's design, patented August 9, 1881.

A: Fusee and emery flint pocket lighter, Great Britain, c. 1890. Brass with chromium plating.
B: Vaudaine's fusee and emery flint pocket lighter and match holder, France, c. 1881. Brass with chromium plating.

••••••••••••

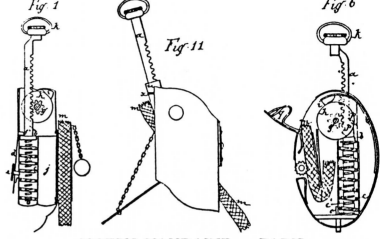

Fig. 1   *Fig. 11*   *Fig. 6*

JOSEPH VAUDAINE ɪɴ PARIS.
Luntenfeuerzeug.

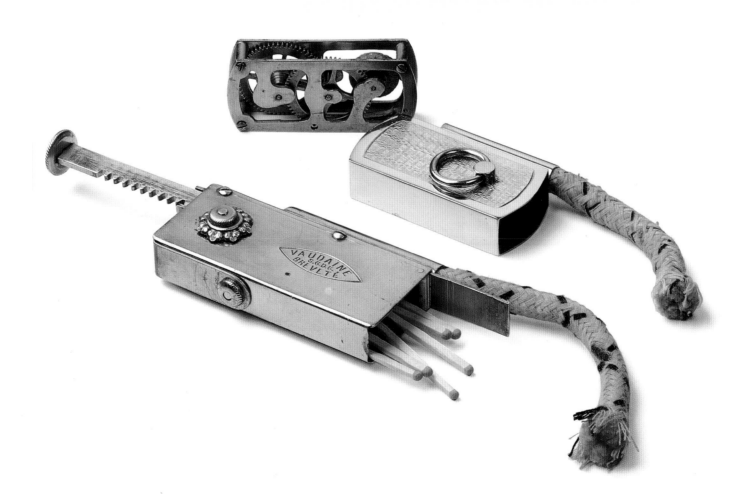

Pyrogan with candle holder, Germany, c. 1880.
Glazed pottery. *Ad and Annie Jansen.*

Pyrogan with cigarette and match holder and tobacco
pot, Germany, c. 1890. Glazed pottery.

··············

*Wind matches by Palmer & Son, Great Britain,
c. 1875. Wood and paper. Ad and Annie Jansen.*

....

*A: Parker candle matches or "five-minute matches" and bedside
lamp, United States, c. 1867. Marked "C. Parker, Meriden,
Connecticut, pat, January 04 1867, USA." Steel plate.
B: Candle matches and bedside lamp, Belgium, c. 1880.
Cardboard and paper. Ad and Annie Jansen.
C: Candle matches and bedside lamp, Belgium, c. 1870.
Leather. These matches and lamps were most often used to light
one's way to the bedroom in the evening.*

....

Matches: the discovery of phosphorus

The numerous, ground-breaking scientific experiments that took place in Europe beginning in the seventeenth century also led to the development of the sulfur sticks, another fire-making device that was to become a valuable commodity in the modern world. The first known matches were the sulfur variety, which had been in use since Roman times. These were made by dipping a wooden splint into a sulfur bath so that a drop remained on the tip, which was then lit by an existing flame or smoldering tinder. Sulfur sticks were later also commercially produced, but they were much thicker than our present-day variety and posed considerable risks. They produced a clear flame when the sulfur hit the smoldering tinder, but gave off noxious, possibly poisonous, smoke. At the very least, those who used sulfur matches to light their pipes were left with a dreadful taste in their mouths.

Phosphorus was another substance that was the subject of centuries of scientific investigation as a possible source material for creating an effective, safe match. It was discovered in 1669 by Henning Brand, an alchemist from Hamburg. Although Brand was a serious scholar, many of his profession were considered charlatans who deceived the public in their often questionable attempts to transmute base metals into gold.

The study of alchemy, which combined elements of science with philosophy and magic, was an ancient tradition dating back to the early Greeks, although by the seventeenth century it was increasingly held in disrepute. Nevertheless, in 1669 Brand made an important contribution to science: while trying to create gold, Brand discovered that when he boiled human urine, the powdery yellow substance which remained in the flask glowed in the dark. He called this "cold fire." Later, a chemist named Johann Elsholz gave it the scientific name "phosphorus," from the Greek word meaning "light-bringer."

Initially, phosphorus was mainly used as a fairground attraction in various conjuring tricks. It was only in England in 1680 that a serious attempt was made to produce phosphorus. Among scientists there was an intuitive feeling that phosphorus might be a more expedient and better fire-maker than flint and steel, though how this extremely flammable and dangerous substance could be mastered remained a mystery for many years.

The first phosphorus match was developed toward the end of the eighteenth century by an Italian doctor named Louis Peyla. He called his invention a Turin candle – a romantic name for fire splints which, when ignited, spewed forth a shower of sparks. Made with highly flammable white

A: Alcohol table lighter with match and cigar cutter by *Geschoss-Fabrik, Germany, c. 1910. Steel, brass, and copper.*
B: *Réchaud alcohol lighter with matches and match holder, France, c. 1900. Gilded brass with chromium plating.*
C: *Réchaud alcohol lighter by La Metropole, Switzerland, c. 1900. Pewter alloy with chromium plating.*

· · · · · · · · · · · ·

phosphorus (the only variety of this substance then known), they had the unfortunate habit of spontaneously bursting into flame if exposed to the sun for too long.

In 1805, a French chemistry student named J.J. Chancel constructed a match head from a wooden splint and sulfur, potassium chlorate, and lycopodium mixed with gum-arabic. The match ignited when the head was dipped into sulfuric acid – an explosive, and highly dangerous, reaction.

An Englishman named Samuel Jones tried to establish an alternative to phosphorus in 1828 with his Promethean matches, made from a mixture of potassium chlorate and sugar rolled into paper. A sealed glass tube was filled with concentrated sulfuric acid, and when the glass was broken with tongs the mixture caught fire. But these matches were not popular, as they were too risky and complicated to use. Moreover, nineteenth-century consumers demanded cheaper, readily available articles.

A year before Jones introduced his Promethean matches, another Englishman named John Walker created a match made with a seven-centimeter splint tipped with a mixture of sulfur, potassium chlorate, and gum arabic, which when rubbed against sandpaper burst into flame. However, even these

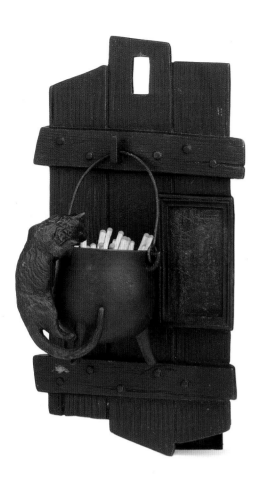

matches were not entirely satisfactory – the head often wore completely down before a light was obtained – and hence people returned to using the earlier, white phosphorus matches. These did have the advantage of burning extremely well, although it was established that they were dangerous for both user and matchmaker. The white phosphorus could penetrate the bones via the bronchial tubes, causing, among other side effects, badly disfigured teeth and jaws. In 1845, another, less toxic type of phosphorus, red phosphorus, was discovered, and a new era began for the match industry. Still, both types of phosphorus remained in use for several more decades; it was not until 1912 that white phosphorus was officially banned throughout Europe.

Safety matches

A Swedish professor, Gustaf Erik Pasch, was the first to make use of the discovery of red phosphorus. Building on John Walker's invention, Pasch replaced the sulfur with red phosphorus. This design was perfected by a Swedish engineer, Johan Edvard Lunström. During the 1855 World Exhibition in Paris, Lunström garnered a great deal of attention when he introduced his "safety matches." They contained no white phosphorus, and were ignited by being rubbed against the side of a box containing harmless, red phosphorus. From that moment on, Sweden became the dominant force in the match industry, and matches were suddenly all the rage across Europe

Wall-mounted pyrogan, United States, c. 1900. Lacquered lead.

A: Match holder, the Netherlands, 1841. Marked "Van Leeuwen, Amsterdam Holland, 1841." Silver. Ad and Annie Jansen.
B: Rowenta match holder, Germany, c. 1935. Brass with chromium plating.
C: Automatic match holder. "Magic", France, c. 1860. Steelplated, chromium plated. In this model, the match is expelled from the holder already lit by the scriber.

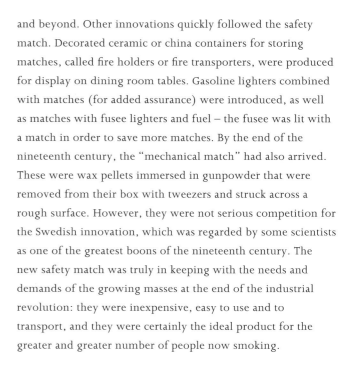

38

Ouragan fusee and flint wheel pocket lighter by Flamidor, France, c. 1941. Marked "75–17." Brass and silver plate.

and beyond. Other innovations quickly followed the safety match. Decorated ceramic or china containers for storing matches, called fire holders or fire transporters, were produced for display on dining room tables. Gasoline lighters combined with matches (for added assurance) were introduced, as well as matches with fusee lighters and fuel – the fusee was lit with a match in order to save more matches. By the end of the nineteenth century, the "mechanical match" had also arrived. These were wax pellets immersed in gunpowder that were removed from their box with tweezers and struck across a rough surface. However, they were not serious competition for the Swedish innovation, which was regarded by some scientists as one of the greatest boons of the nineteenth century. The new safety match was truly in keeping with the needs and demands of the growing masses at the end of the industrial revolution: they were inexpensive, easy to use and to transport, and they were certainly the ideal product for the greater and greater number of people now smoking.

The Crimean War and the burgeoning cigarette industry

Until the Crimean War (1854–56), tobacco use in Europe was largely limited to chewing or snuff-taking, or smoking a pipe or cigar. Cigarettes existed, but they were primarily smoked in parts of eastern Europe and the Balkans. All this changed during the Crimean conflict. The French, British, and Sardinian soldiers fighting on the front to help Turkey in its struggle against Russia found it extremely inconvenient to have to carry their smoking gear with them. Often, their pipes did not survive the daily battles, as the soldiers had to drag themselves along the ground on their stomachs for considerable distances. On the other hand, the Turkish and Russian soldiers held thin straws in their mouths, which they effortlessly drew on, even when skirmishes were breaking out, their thick, satisfying clouds of smoke mingling with the smoke of the cannons. Returning European soldiers were full of stories from the battlefield concerning the remarkable pleasures of smoking. The overwhelming winner of the Crimean War seems to have been the cigarette industry, for from this time on, cigarette smoking grew alongside the manufacture of lighters and matches.

A: Roll-up fusee and flint wheel pocket lighter, France, c. 1920. Marked "breveté 75-81." Brass with chromium plating.
B: Roll-up fusee and flint wheel pocket lighter , Austria, c. 1920. Brass with chromium plating.

....

A: Fusee and flint wheel pocket lighter, France, c. 1911. Brass with chromium plating. Imprinted with a French tax seal.
B: Fusee and flint wheel table lighter, Spain, c. 1970. Brass with chromium plating.
C: Tempête fusee and flint wheel pocket lighter, France, c. 1914. Brass with chromium plating.

....

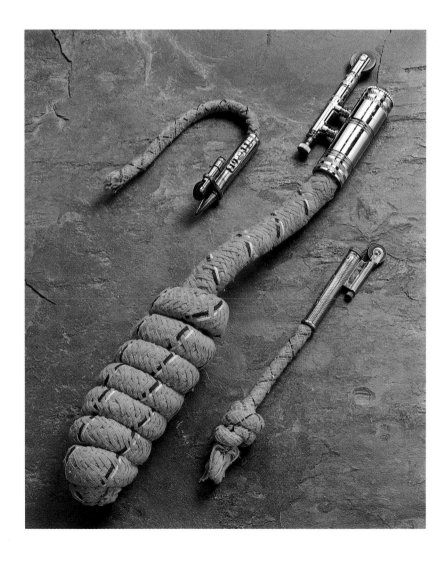

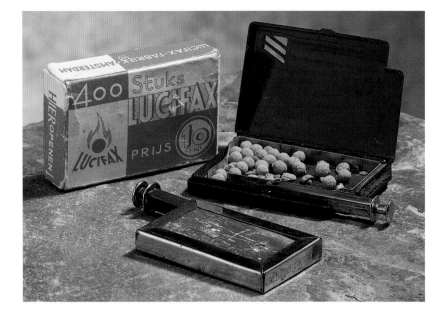

Super gasoline and flint wheel lighter with match holder, Belgium, c. 1930. Lacquered aluminum.

Opposite: *A*: Wick, gasoline, and flint wheel pocket lighter, France, c. 1920. Brass with chromium plating.
B: Feudor wick, gasoline, and flint wheel pocket lighter, France, c. 1939. Marked "69-2" and imprinted with a French tax seal. Brass with chromium plating.

A: Lucifax match lighter with wax and phosphorus pellets, the Netherlands, c. 1935. Bakelite and steel plate. This model was marketed as both a match and a lighter; it was promoted as safe and reliable because it was not made of wood. Lucifax was registered as a trademark in the Netherlands on August 20, 1936.
B: Jon Wonder Light match lighter with wax and phosphorus pellets, Great Britain, c. 1928. Steel plate with chromium plating.

Pocket lighter by the Hahway Company, Germany, c. 1915. Brass with chromium plating.
A gasoline and flint wheel lighter, a fusee and flint wheel lighter, and a gasoline lighter that includes a flint and a wand for striking the flint that is screwed into the bottom of the lighter.

4

A CAVALCADE OF NEW PRODUCTS

Innovation and Progress

Gasoline table lighter with flint striker, Austria, c. 1915. Lacquered lead.

Gasoline and flint wheel pocket lighter, Germany, c. 1935. Brass with chromium plating and lacquered.
....

The 1900 World Exhibition in Paris seemed to exemplify the spirit of progress and competition that characterized the turn of the new century. Technical wonders, such as the 500-horsepower engine, were on view, along with the first automobiles and the latest bicycles. Indeed, the thirst for novelty was evident everywhere at the dawn of the twentieth century.

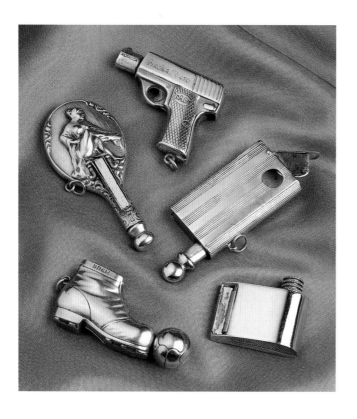

A: Pirona gasoline pocket lighter with flint striker, model 410, Germany, c. 1920. Brass and alpaca.

B: Karl Wieden gasoline pocket lighter with flint striker, model 390, Germany, c. 1910. Brass and alpaca. This lighter reverses to a hand mirror.

C: Sarasto gasoline pocket lighter with flint striker, model 403, Germany, c. 1920. Brass and alpaca. This lighter contains a cigar cutter.

D: Gasoline pocket lighter with flint striker, Germany, c. 1920. Brass and alpaca.

E: Wrist-fix gasoline pocket lighter with flint striker by Ristex, Great Britain, c. 1947. Brass with chromium plating.

Ristex advertisement, Tobacco magazine, September 1947.

"Auermetall" gasoline table lighter with flint striker, Austria, patented November 27, 1906. Brass.

New art forms, such as photography and film were flowering, while painting and sculpture were becoming increasingly abstract and stylized; a rash of new movements, including Art Nouveau and expressionism, signaled the arrival of a new cultural era.

Inevitably, the industrial landscape was also changing dramatically. Factory chimneys that belched smoke were seen less and less, as alternative forms of energy, such as oil, gas, and electricity, replaced coal and wood burning, and furnaces were increasingly streamlined. With these new, more efficient sources of energy came a growing consumer demand for products that provided comfort and convenience. The modern automobile and aircraft industries began to take shape, and new technologies were perfected and applied to the production of a wide spectrum of goods. In every field, inventors were busy expanding upon the achievements of the industrial revolution, and they hurried to acquire patents for their innovations. The race to profit from the proliferation of new goods was on; ambitious entrepreneurs vied for a piece of these growing markets, from household products to automobiles to lighters.

As the century wore on, more and better lighters were sold to a broader and broader public. The lighter virtually became an indispensable item in the home and at work, as well as a valuable promotional gift, a souvenir of a special trip or event, and even as a keepsake or collectible.

Carl Auer von Welsbach

One outstanding early twentieth-century innovator was an Austrian chemist named Carl Auer von Welsbach, who devoted his life to science, specializing in the study of lanthanides, or rare earth elements, such as lanthanum. Auer discovered that oxides from lanthanides become incandescent when heated. This led to the invention of a protective mantle for gaslight, a device which allowed for a considerable increase in the intensity of the light itself. He was also credited with improving electric light by using cerium, another rare earth element, in electric light filaments. In 1903, Auer made the important discovery that ferro cerium, an amalgam of iron and cerium, produces powerful sparks when it is scratched. This alloy, which later became known as Auer metal, was adapted with great success as flints in cigarette lighters. When a hard object is drawn or scratched sharply across them, relatively high energy, or heat, is released in a short period of time. Auer based his invention on the work of Joseph Vaudaine, whose 1878 lighter contained a similar "flint". The vital difference was that Vaudaine's design used an emery stone, a natural material fashioned into a "flint" in the form of a wheel. The drawback of this lighter was that both the wheel and the iron it rubbed against quickly wore down. Nonetheless,

45

Two gasoline table lighters with flint strikers, Austria,
c. 1910. Lacquered lead.

•••••••••••

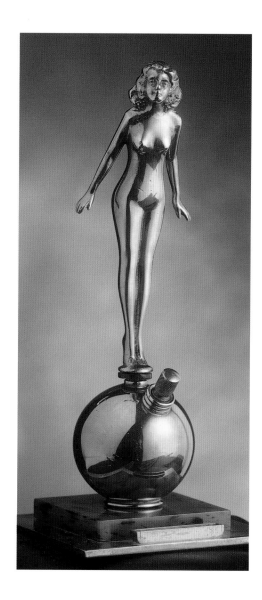

Vaudaine did patent his invention, for it was far superior to the fire steel, iron, and pyrite then in use. The emery wheel lighter was no match for the benefits of Auer metal, however, which required a much less complex mechanism to produce a flame. In a lighter with the flint made with Auer metal, one brief movement produced a number of sparks, compared to several spins of Vaudaine's emery wheel. Because of this invention, Auer, who acquired a patent for his metal on July 27, 1903, made perhaps the greatest contribution to the development of the lighter as we know it today.

In 1907, Carl Auer von Welsbach opened the first factory to make Auer metal, Treibacher Chemischer Werke, in Vienna. TCW initially produced the metal in blocks, so that customers had to cut their own flints. But because this was an age that demanded convenience, manufacturers wanted a more efficient product. Soon, factory-made scrapers were being produced, first with one tooth (the scriber), then several teeth (the file), then many teeth set in a simple mechanical form. The final innovation was a file of teeth that was rolled up into round flint wheel. This was activated by a simple thumb movement, much like the one we use on lighters today; the action of scraping the wheel along the flint produced a shower of sparks. The flint, in cylindrical form was enclosed in a tube contiguous to the flint wheel. The necessary pressure between the flint and the wheel was produced by a spring located below the flint in the flint tube. The teeth on the outside of the flint wheel had to be tough, or the flint would wear down too quickly. Conversely, the inside had to be relatively soft to prevent the wheel from breaking.

Gasoline table lighters with flint striker, Great Britain, c. 1930. Brass with chromium plating and lacquered steel base.

Gasoline table lighter with flint striker, Great Britain, c. 1939. Gilded brass with plastic foot.

Gondola gasoline table lighter with flint striker by
Parker, Great Britain, 1937. Pewter alloy, brass, and
enamel with chromium plating.

A: Ewiges Zündholtz gasoline pocket lighter with flint
striker, Germany, c. 1915. Brass with chromium
plating.
B: Gasoline pocket lighter with flint striker, Germany,
c. 1920. Brass with chromium plating.
C: Knirps gasoline pocket lighter with flint striker,
Germany, c. 1915. Brass with chromium plating.
D: Fire Chief fusee pocket lighter with flint striker,
United States, c. 1930. Plastic and metal alloy with
chromium plating.

....

Four rare lighters in which the flint is in the wand and
the striking surface is on the lighter. The Fire Chief
lighter, in the foreground, has both the fusee and the wand within the
lighter; the flint striker surface is drawn across the wand. In the other
models, the wick is in the wand.

....

Flint system lighters usually operated either by means of the strike method,
whereby the flint is simply scratched with a steel point or scraped across a
file, or by the file method, which uses either a straight file or a semi- or
fully rotating round file to produce a spark.

....

A: *Airflam methanol pocket lighter with platinum catalyst, Germany, c. 1952. Anodized aluminum.*
B: *Airflam methanol pocket lighter with platinum catalyst, Germany, c. 1952. Anodized aluminum. This lighter won a gold medal at the 1952 World Exhibition in Luxembourg.*

C: *Airflam methanol lighter with platinum catalyst, table model, Germany, c. 1952. Ceramic and anodized aluminum.*

··········

A: C. E. W. methanol pocket lighter with platinum catalyst, United States, patented 1907. Silver, 521.
B: Platina methanol pocket lighter with platinum catalyst, Germany, c. 1907. Brass with chromium plating.
C: Lytic methanol pocket lighter with platinum catalyst, Great Britain, c. 1910. Marked "C.P. Marshall-W'Pton Ltd, England." Brass with chromium plating.
D: Hera methanol pocket lighter with platinum catalyst, Germany, c. 1910. Marked "Foreign." Brass with chromium plating.
E: Vulcan methanol pocket lighter with platinum catalyst, Germany, c. 1910. Brass with chromium plating.

A: Lektrolite methanol pocket lighter with platinum catalyst, United States, c, 1947. Metal alloy with chromium plating.
B: L'Obelisque methanol pocket lighter with platinum catalyst, France, c. 1935. Gilded brass.
C: Lektrolite methanol pocket lighter with platinum catalyst, United States, patented 1907. Brass with chromium plating.

Lektrolite advertisement featuring Al Jolson, Esquire magazine, June 1936.

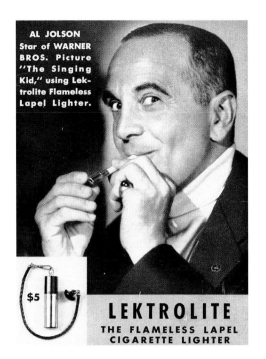

AL JOLSON Star of WARNER BROS. Picture "The Singing Kid," using Lektrolite Flameless Lapel Lighter.

$5

LEKTROLITE
THE FLAMELESS LAPEL
CIGARETTE LIGHTER

The market

Following the discovery of Auer metal, lighters were being produced all over Europe. They were often made from some readily available material. On the inside was cotton wool soaked with gasoline, which was in contact with a wick housed in a tube that protruded from the lighter shell. By pulling the tube out of the lighter and scraping its steel tip along the flint – as one would a match – a spark was produced that ignited the wick. Austria was the primary manufacturer of lighters during the early 1900s, as this country had a virtual monopoly on flints. Lighters made to resemble people or animals were particularly popular at this time.

As smoking became more and more commonplace, lighters were increasingly in demand; new markets sprang up all over the world during the first quarter of the century. Eager for a share of these markets, many European factories that were

A: Pyrus gasoline and electric spark wall lighter,
France, c. 1935. Bakelite.
B: Elektro Lucifer gasoline and electric spark wall
lighter by Homor, Zaandam, the Netherlands,
c. 1935. Bakelite and wood with red lacquer.

A: Glopoint methanol pocket lighter with platinum
catalyst by Lektrolite, United States, c. 1936. Bakelite
and brass with gold plating.
B: Flameless methanol pocket lighter with platinum
catalyst by Lektrolite, United States, c. 1941.
Bakelite.

···········

already using metal to make their products began producing lighters as well. Standard designs for everyday objects were adjusted for the manufacture of these new, popular products. Hollow ornaments were packed with gasoline-drenched cotton wool, a striker was attached, Auer metal was added, and an instant, fashionable lighter was produced. Even the most whimsical, incongruous items were adapted: in Switzerland, lighters were made that incorporated a clock, while in Austria and Germany, they included a powder compact, musical box, or perfume bottle. The eau de cologne lighter was a particularly original creation of this era. It worked the same way as those that used gasoline and a flint wheel, but was filled with light perfume, rather than the usual gasoline, so that it gave off a pleasant fragrance. Women, who were smoking more and more – partly due to the recent suffrage movements, and partly because of the increasing influence of the glamorous, smoke-filled world of the movies – were especially taken with a device that functioned both as a lighter and a perfume dispenser. A related version was a lighter that contained a perfumed sponge to counteract the unpleasant smell of the gasoline; and another popular design combined a lighter and a cigarette case. An increasing variety of materials were used in manufacturing these lighters, including copper, brass, gold, silver, Bakelite, and even leather.

A: Depro "eau de cologne" pocket lighter with flint striker by Voss-Industrie, Berlin-Neukölln, Germany, c. 1950.
B: Novitas Sales alcohol and flint wheel pocket lighter, United States, c. 1930. Brass with chromium plating.
C: Alcohol and flint wheel pocket lighter, United States, Pat. 1922. Brass with chromium plating.

....

A: Couic gasoline and electric spark wall lighter, Germany, c. 1935. Bakelite.
B: Stohr gasoline and electric spark wall lighter, Germany, c. 1940. Bakelite.

....

Gasoline and electric spark wall lighter, possibly Belgium, c. 1935. Wood and brass with chromium plating.

A: Wit gasoline and electric spark wall lighter marked Breveté, Sans Garantie Du Gouvernement, France, c. 1922. Steel plate and brass with chromium plating.
B: Jalumé gasoline and electric spark wall lighter marked Bté, S.G.D.G., France, c. 1920. Steel plate and brass with chromium plating.

············

The first brand name lighters

During the first quarter of the century, manufacturers began marketing lighters under specific brand names. Industry leaders were eager to distinguish themselves by making a recognizable, quality product. Thorens, a prominent Swiss manufacturer of music boxes, produced distinctive lighters that were known for having the same mechanical precision and technical refinement associated with the Swiss clock industry. IMCO, an Austrian firm run by J. Meister & Co., began specializing in lighters in 1918. Between 1920 and 1930, IMCO developed six new models designed with the now-famous IMCO shield to protect the flame from the wind. IMCO not only had an innovative edge over its competitors, but also provided good value; its well-known Triplex model was considered the Volkswagen of lighters.

The leading French brand in the early 1900s was Flamidor, the flagship design of a Paris lighter firm. The company began manufacturing this lighter in 1912, but the Flamidor really took off after 1935, when Janvier Quercia became director of the company. The names Flamidor and Quercia became so inextricably linked that later, even

collectors thought Quercia had designed the brand himself.

Along with metal producers, manufacturers of pipes and tobacco products were also eager to increase their reputations and revenues by developing their own signature lighters. In 1928, French pipe maker Albert Alphonse Lancel began making lighters under the Lancel name, while in England lighters were produced and trademarked by the ORLIK, CIVIC, and OPL (Oppenheimer Pipes Limited) companies. In Germany, the Karl Wieden factory produced lighters under the KW and, later, Ka Wee trademarks; these two brands became extremely popular with collectors.

Another highly sought-after German trademark was the JBELO lighter. This brand was produced by Julius and Benno Lowenthal, two highly successful Jewish brothers. In 1933, the Lowenthals fled Nazi Germany and settled in Britain, where they both continued making and selling lighters. Benno's trademark was Benlow Limited, and Julius founded Colibri Lighters Limited. They both became fierce competitors of London-based Alfred Dunhill, who originally ran an exclusive tobacconist shop, but had started marketing lighters shortly before World War I because of increasing consumer demand.

A: Kiya electro/glowing filament table lighter with push-button mechanism, perfume spray, and ash trays, Germany, c. 1930. Ceramic and Bakelite. This lighter includes a lamp and a small tray with perfume above it; as the lamp heats up, the perfume evaporates.

B: Electro-glowing filament table lighter with push-button mechanism, Germany, patented 1923. Lacquered lead. When a button on the back of the top of the lighter was pushed, the coiled element on the top glowed.

Made in 110/140 volt and, later, in 110/220 volt versions, these electro wall or bistro lighters were used both at home and in public places such as bars and restaurants. All were ignited by means of a spark produced by a striking wand. Some were connected directly to an electrical source via a cable, while others were inserted into electric sockets. In model 5030, the electric wire and the wand are uninsulated; in a later version, model 10198, both elements are covered. In models 5458 and 26269 the gasoline tank is incorporated into the wand; a spark was produced when the wand was taken out of its holder. In all other models, the wand, which also contains the wick, is suspended in a separate gasoline tank.

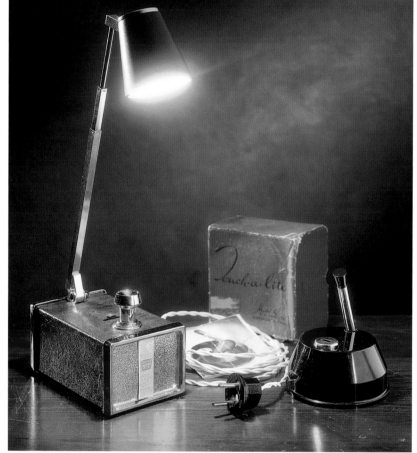

Gasoline and battery/glowing filament table lighter, Great Britain, c. 1931. Wood and brass with chromium plating.

• • • • • • • • • • • •

 The Ludwig Zwilling company in Walldorf, Germany patented a pocket lighter with a battery/glowing filament in May 1929, though it remains unclear if the design was ever actually produced. On October 21, 1949, Hans Wilhelm Fischbach applied for a patent for a similar lighter that included a torch, which was later marketed in Germany under the Fumalux trademark. Similar lighters were also made in Great Britain and marketed under such names as Magna, Pyrolux, and Nuradon. The early versions ran on Rulag batteries, while a later model, produced in 1956 under the Duralux name, required Penlight batteries.

• • • • • • • • • • • •

A: Casco electro/glowing filament table lighter, model LAC-2, United States, c. 1950. Brass with chromium plating and leather edging. This model operated the same way as a lighter in a car.
B: P. X. Fox electro/glowing filament table lighter, Great Britain, c. 1950. Bakelite and brass with chromium plating. In this model, the wand was filled with gasoline-soaked cotton wool and a wick; when the wand was removed from its holder, the filament automatically glowed and could then be used to ignite the wand.

• • • • • • • • • • • •

A: Fumalux gasoline and battery/glowing filament
pocket lighter and lamp, model FL-400, Germany,
patented 1949. Brass with chromium plating.
B: Dura-lux gasoline and battery/glowing filament
pocket lighter and lamp by Fumalux, Germany,
c. 1957. Brass with chromium plating.
C: Fumalux gasoline and battery/glowing filament
pocket lighter and lamp, model FL-2, Germany,
patented 1949. Brass with chromium plating.
D: Dura-lux gasoline and flint wheel pocket lighter and
lamp, model DL-810, Japan, c. 1965. Brass with
chromium plating.

. . . .

Advertisement for Rulag batteries.

Hand-built gasoline and battery spark table lighter,
the Netherlands, c. 1935. Wood and plastic.
Hand-built models were quite varied; this one was
ignited by an electric spark and recharged via a bobbin
device that resembled those used to operate doorbells.

. . . .

A: Auth gasoline and semi-rotating flint wheel table lighter, Germany, patented 1924. Bakelite and brass with chromium plating.
This lighter was re-introduced during the 1950s in various colored plastic versions.
B: Guinn gasoline and semi-rotating flint wheel table lighter by SE Guinn Manufacturing Co., Johnson City, Tennessee, c. 1930. Lacquered bronze.

C: Gasoline and semi-rotating flint wheel table lighter, Germany, c. 1930. Lacquered brass.
D: Gasoline and semi-rotating flint wheel table lighter, Germany, patented 1924. Steel and brass with chromium plating; wood base.
E: Gasoline and semi-rotating flint wheel table lighter, Germany, c. 1920. Brass.

···········

In the United States, Louis V. Aronson, founder of the Ronson Company, marketed the first American-made brand name lighter. As a young man, Aronson had been a highly inventive student, one of whose specialties was electroplating. He patented the process and then sold it under the condition that he could continue to use his own patent free of charge. Then Aronson built Art Metal Works, a factory in New Jersey that produced Art Deco lamps, ashtrays, bookends, and pipe racks. After the development of modern lighter flint in Europe, Aronson's company adapted and marketed their products as lighters. In 1928, Aronson took out a patent for the Ronson Banjo, the first fully automatic lighter, which combined all the steps previously needed to spark a flame into a single, simple movement. When the Ronson Banjo was actuated, a flame instantly appeared; when the lid and spring were released, the flame went out. Numerous other Ronson lighters based on the Banjo's design were developed over the years, and many of these are also now highly prized by collectors. Largely due to the ingenuity of manufacturers like Aronson and his European colleagues, the lighter was fast becoming a stylish and popular gift. By the 1930s, many people were buying lighters and having them engraved with names or commemorative dates for family members, friends, and business associates.

A: Mosda gasoline and semi-rotating flint wheel pocket lighter, Great Britain, c. 1933. Brass with chromium plating.
B: Premier gasoline and semi-rotating flint wheel pocket lighter, Great Britain, c. 1930. Brass with chromium plating.
C: Bruma gasoline and semi-rotating flint wheel pocket lighter, Germany, c. 1930. Brass with chromium plating.

Advertisement for Colibri lighters.

The earliest flint lighters used a semi-rotating wheel, which wore down quickly, as it scraped across the flint during both active and non-active revolutions. In some models, teeth were applied only to the section of the wheel that was used; in other versions, only half of a wheel was installed. Later, manufacturers began using wheels that had four holes; when the first quarter of the wheel had worn down, the next section was used.

Two Stambu gasoline and semi-rotating flint wheel lighters, Germany, c. 1930. Brass with chromium plating.

A: *Abdulla gasoline and semi-rotating flint wheel pocket lighter, France, c. 1929. Brass with chromium plating.*
B: *Abdulla gasoline and semi-rotating flint wheel pocket lighter, France, c.1932. Brass with chromium plating and leather edging.*
C: *Gasoline and semi-rotating flint wheel pocket lighter, Germany, c. 1930. Marked "D.R.G.M. Foreign." Brass with chromium plating.*

Gasoline lighters

Twentieth-century gasoline lighters can roughly be divided into three types: manual, semi-automatic, and automatic. Although petroleum and its by-products had been known to man since the time of the ancient Sumerians, their potential as important natural resources was not discovered until the late nineteenth century, when the first oil companies starting drilling for and distributing oil as fuel. In the United States, the first person to recognize the enormous potential of petroleum was John D. Rockefeller, whose Standard Oil firm became one of the world's largest oil companies. Overseas, the Royal Dutch Petroleum Company, founded in 1890 (which became part of the Royal Shell Group in 1907), dominated much of the European market.

Gasoline was considered a waste product of crude oil until the arrival of the automobile industry, which transformed it into one of the most valuable commodities in the modern world. Scientists and entrepreneurs began experimenting with gasoline to see if it could be used as a fuel for new products and machines other than cars, including lighters. The first manual gasoline lighter involved opening the lighter to operate the flint wheel, then closing it to extinguish the flame. This model was followed by the semi-automatic gasoline lighter, which when first opened also activated the flint wheel, and when closed stretched a spring so that the lighter could be opened the next time by simply pressing a button. The fully automatic gasoline lighter, the most sophisticated lighter of this type, opened and lit up with a single push of the thumb, then shut when the pressure was released, simultaneously closing off the tiny gasoline tank and extinguishing the flame.

Electric lighters

The electric lighter has a much more complex history than the gasoline-fueled model. Electric friction was first discovered around 600 BC by the Greek philosopher Thales of Miletus, who found that when amber, a fossil resin, was rubbed, it

Gasoline and semi-rotating flint wheel wall lighter marked Breveté S.G.D.G., France, c. 1925. Bakelite.

Gasoline and semi-rotating flint wheel table lighter, Germany, c. 1920. Brass.

60

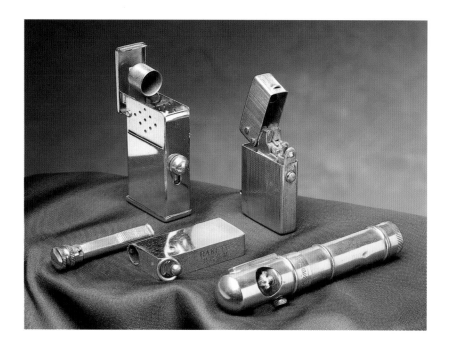

A: Lesansroulette gasoline and flint grater pocket lighter, France, c. 1930. Brass with chromium plating.
B: Always gasoline and flint grater pocket lighter, Germany, c. 1910. Brass with chromium plating.
C: "Rakété", Germany, c. 1920. Brass, chromium plated.
D: Hinora gasoline and flint grater pocket lighter, model 149, Germany, c. 1935. Brass.

A: Transfo flint wheel pocket lighter by D'Alton Co., France, c. 1950. Aluminum and brass with chromium plating.
B: Garidon flint wheel pocket lighter by New Device, Japan, c. 1985. Plastic and brass with gold plating.

• • • • • • • • • • •

These two unique lighters produce sparks by means of either a rotating lever or a wheel; the flint sparks ignite the cigarette. The slide cover on the Garidon lighter closes off the hole where the spark is produced.

• • • • • • • • • • •

A: *Omega Super gasoline and flint wheel pocket lighter, Japan, c. 1949. Brass with chromium plating and plastic edging. This lighter is imprinted with an Argentine tax stamp.*
B: *Gasoline and fusee pocket lighter with exploding ignition and cap tape and hammer, France, c. 1896. Brass with chromium plating.*

Left to right: two Belgian tax seals; three French tax seals.

. . . .

would attract extremely light objects, such as feathers. In 70 AD, the Roman author Pliny the Elder described similar experiments in his famous work, Natural History. Formal investigation of such phenomena did not begin again until the seventeenth century, when English scientist William Gilbert, who also worked with amber, discovered the difference between electric and magnetic attraction. Around 1736, French chemist Charles François Du Fay determined that electrical charges either attract or repel each other depending on whether they are different or the same – like charges repel; different charges attract. Moreover, Du Fay suggested that electricity consisted of two types of liquid, which he termed "vitreous" and "resinous". This finding led to the invention of the Leyden jar, a device created in 1745 by both a German clergyman, E. Georg von Kleist, and University of Leyden professor Pieter van Musschenbroek, working independently of each other. Their mutual discovery was that a glass jar filled with water and charged with a friction source could store the electrical charge for later use.

The English team of Dr. John Bevis and Sir William Watson later lined a Leyden jar with tinfoil on both the outside and inside, thereby creating a vessel that could store an electrical charge strong enough to produce sparks which could explode gunpowder or light alcohol on fire. Watson further discovered that electricity can travel almost instantaneously along a wire about two miles long, and, contrary to Du Fay's findings, he suggested that electricity consisted of only one type of fluid. Watson's one-fluid model for electricity was supported by Benjamin Franklin, the eighteenth-century American statesman and inventor whose own experiments with natural electrical charges led to his invention of the lightening rod.

Nineteenth-century scientists expanded on Du Fay's, Watson's, and Franklin's discoveries in every direction. In 1820, the electromagnet was invented in England by William Sturgeon; Scottish physicist James Clark Maxwell determined the speed of electromagnetic waves; and in 1897, another Englishman, Sir Joseph J. Thomson discovered the basic component of an electrical current, a negatively charged particle called an electron. The discovery of the electron provided the basis for the tremendous advances in electronics

that took place at the turn of the century, such as the invention of the induction motor, the light bulb, and the telephone. Soon, scientists were searching for ways to apply electricity to the multitude of other new products being created, including lighters. Some electric lighters were connected directly to a central supply of electricity and fixed to a wall, and others were made with a plug that would fit into any electric socket, while still others came with their own separate plug and cord. They were employed to either ignite the lighter fuel or, with a glowing filament (a conductive thread), light a cigarette, cigar, or pipe.

Battery lighters

Experiments with electricity also spurred the development of the battery-powered lighter. Although findings from excavations around Baghdad have suggested that electricity-producing, or galvanic, cells may have been in use in that region as much as two thousand years ago, it was an Italian scientist named Count Alessandro Volta who is credited with inventing the first device to produce a steady current of electricity. Around 1800, Volta was working on the findings of his colleague Luigi Galvani, who had recently discovered that tension exists between two distinct metals when they are submerged in conductive solutions. Volta suspected that the reason for this was a reaction by which chemical energy is converted into electrical energy (which is why galvanic cells are now also called electrochemical cells). He placed different types of metals in piles between pads that had been immersed

A: Methane counter lighter, c. 1920. Bronze with gold plating.
B: Methane counter lighter, the Netherlands, c. 1925. Brass with gold plating.
C: Gasoline and flint grater wall-mounted lighter, Germany, c. 1910. Brass and steel with chromium plating.

Gas tobacconist's lighter, Great Britain, c. 1890. Bronze. This type of tobacconist's lighter was connected to a central supply of gas and burned continuously in the shop. Splinters were used to transport the flame to a pipe or cigar.

Advertisement poster for Rodenstock.

RODENSTOCK
MODELL *Lord*

Mico smoking stand with electro/glowing filament
lighter, United States, c. 1925. Lacquered steel, glass,
and brass with chromium plating. This push-button
model includes an ash tray and a cigarette tray.

....

in acid or salt solutions, and the piles created a steady current of electricity between them – the battery was born. Other early efforts to create an electric battery included experiments that involved simultaneously discharging electrical currents in two Leyden jars.

During the early twentieth century, many attempts were made to produce an efficient battery lighter, but few of these designs got off the ground, such as the model made with zinc and carbon that could never be produced in the handy pocket-size consumers wanted. A patent for a battery lighter was taken out in 1929, but it was not until twenty years later that a successful model was produced by Hans Wilhelm Fishbach, whose Fumalux design became the most popular battery lighter. Made with a battery-powered wire filament, the Fumalux was able to compete with the gasoline and flint wheel lighters already in use. The Fumalux system was launched under various brand names around the world, and operated along the same lines as an electric model: either the current from the battery heated a filament so that a cigarette or the lighter fluid could then be lit from the glow, or, as in the Fumalux design, the glowing filament lit the lighter fluid.

Eldred gasoline and electric spark counter lighter,
United States, c. 1919. Wood and brass with
chromium plating. Boris and Maya Rubin.

....

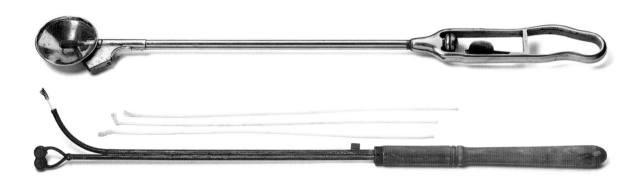

Methanol lighters

At the turn of the century, other lighters began to appear that
used methanol instead of gasoline for fuel. In the same way
that platinum can act as a catalyst to inflame hydrogen, this
precious metal can also be used to ignite methyl alcohol, better
known today as methanol. In methanol lighters, several paper-
thin platinum wires held a small pellet of extremely porous
platinum black. No mechanism was needed to produce a flame:
the lighter was simply opened and a spontaneous combustion
occurred. These lighters were extremely inexpensive to
produce, and between 1905 and 1910, the market was flooded
with various models; at one point during this period between
thirty and forty patents for methanol lighters were requested.
However, their popularity was relatively short-lived because
they were found to be quite dangerous. Not only is methanol a
poisonous substance, but these lighters presented a serious fire
hazard, as users could easily be set alight. Demand for
methanol lighters quickly dwindled, although around 1930
and again in 1950, there was a strange but marked revival of
interest in them. A methanol lighter, the Airflam, was awarded
a gold medal at the 1952 International Fair in Luxembourg. In
retrospect, this almost smacks of a posthumous honor, for
apart from being a curiosity and a memento from a period of
great experimentation, the methanol lighter no longer had any
special significance or practical use.

A: Flint wheel oven lighter, France, c. 1950.
Aluminum and wood.
B: Begra flint wheel oven lighter, possibly Germany,
c. 1947. Metal alloy.
C: Atto flint wheel oven lighter, Switzerland, c. 1950.
Aluminum and brass.

A: Gas lamp lighter with flint grater, marked
"Safety", United States, patented 1909. Brass with
chromium plating. Boris and Maya Rubin.
B: Gas lamp and candle lighter with taper, United
States, patented February 27, 1883. Steel plate and
wood. Boris and Maya Rubin.

....

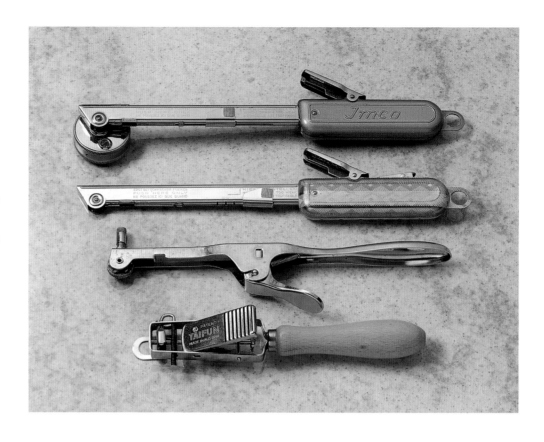

A: Funkmeister gasoline and flint wheel oven lighter by Imco, Austria, 1950. Steel with chromium plating and lacquer. This lighter includes a wick and a gasoline tank.

B: Funkmeister flint wheel oven lighter by Imco, Austria, 1949. Steel and chrome.

C: Fabo flint wheel oven lighter, France, c. 1950. Steel with chromium plating.

D: Taifun flint wheel oven lighter, Austria, c. 1960. Wood and steel with chromium plating.

A: Hand-built flint wheel oven lighter, Great Britain, c. 1920. Steel, brass, and wood.

B: Flint wheel oven lighter, marked "75-4", France, c. 1935. Steel plate and wood. Imprinted with a French tax seal.

Brochure for Rotral.

A: Flint wheel oven lighter, Germany, c. 1960. Steel
with chromium plating and plastic. A holder for a
spare flint is located in the lighter case.
B: Shoot-A-Lite flint wheel oven lighter, United States,
c. 1960. Steel with chromium plating.
C: Flint wheel oven lighter, marked "77-1", France,
c. 1935. Steel with chromium plating. Imprinted with
a French tax seal.

A: Plenid battery/glowing filament oven lighter,
possibly Japan, c. 1960. Brass with chromium
plating.
B: Mechaniece electric spark oven lighter France,
c. 1935. Bakelite and brass with chromium plating.

....

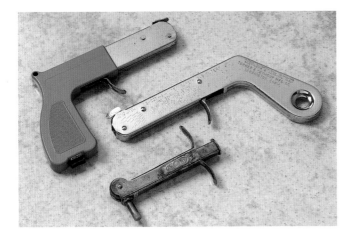

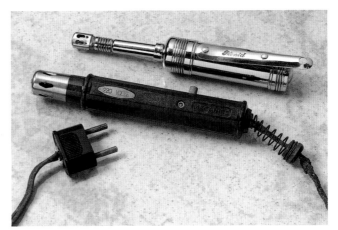

Market regulation

As soon as lucrative markets existed for lighters and matches, government agencies began to intervene with the production, importing, and exporting of these products. In 1872, France became the first European country to establish a state monopoly on the production and selling of matches. The previous year, legislation had been introduced that defined all fire-making devices as belonging to a single category of goods, so that when lighters were developed toward the end of the century, they also fell under the state monopoly. This worked to the government's advantage until 1903, when ferro-cerium was discovered in Austria, and better lighters could be produced outside of France and imported. As a result, the export of French lighters declined considerably. It was not until December 1910 that the French lighter was withdrawn from the state monopoly, and just a year later, France became the second European country, after Germany, to levy a special lighter tax; all lighters sold in France were required to carry a special seal indicating that the tax had been paid.

The new legislation further stipulated that a license be obtained for the production and importing of lighters, although those made for export were exempt. The absurd complexity of this law was evident in that it included a separate ruling stating that if old, worn-out parts of a lighter had to be replaced, the new devices were not taxable. And, lighters that were permanently connected to the French network of gas street lighting were also tax exempt, while those that were separate but sometimes used to light the same lamps were not.

Aside from a few strictly prescribed exemptions, lighters could also only be sold in state tobacconists. One such exemption included the promotional lighters that firms gave away to those who bought considerable quantities of their goods. This practice created a huge tax evasion: boxes of worthless merchandise were sold in order for customers to obtain promotional lighters. France's tax policy was so far-reaching that foreigners visiting the country could bring in no more than two lighters, and had to have these stamped for identification.

Other countries also imposed taxes on lighters, although each pursued its own policy. Beginning in 1923, Belgium, like France, required a metal tax seal on all lighters; in Italy and several South American countries, lighters had to carry a tax stamp similar to the revenue band found on cigarette packages. Most countries eliminated lighter taxes during the 1950s and 1960s, with one prominent exception: the United Kingdom retained its lighter tax until January 1, 1993, when all trade barriers within the European Economic Community were abolished.

Evermatch gasoline and flint wheel lighter, Sweden, c. 1933. Brass with chromium plating and enamel. This lighter was refilled via a tube at the lighter base. The tube was suspended in the gasoline and a round button was pressed to pump up the fuel. Additional fuel could also be pumped to the wick if needed — as, for instance, under windy conditions.

The British lighter tax was both long-lasting and far-reaching. The original tax had been levied on the lighter's ignition device; this legislation then later applied to imported ignition parts, or piezo elements, brought in from Japan during the late 1960s. Fifty pence (around eighty cents) per element went to the state treasury, which made importing these parts very costly for lighter manufacturers. Eventually, the manufacturers reached a compromise with the state revenue office: upon arrival in the U.K., imported piezo elements were held in bonded warehouses until they were actually needed at the lighter factories; the tax was then levied on those parts that were released from the warehouses.

Tobacconists

Regardless of the various scientific and legal obstacles the lighter has faced over the years, the age-old practice of smoking a cigar, pipe, or cigarette has always engendered an atmosphere of contentment and civility. Native Americans smoked peace pipes since before the colonial era, and nineteenth-century gentlemen on both sides of the Atlantic ritually smoked cigars and drank port after dinner, often donning special smoking jackets. The purchasing of tobacco goods became an elaborate ritual in itself, and proprietors of the tobacconists, or "small emporiums for smoking," devoted themselves to accommodating their customers as fully as possible, often providing detailed information on the latest smoking trends and newest smoking products. Along with various types of tobacco, tobacconists also typically carried lighters, matches, ashtrays, and other specialty items. A particularly popular product of the 1930s was the luxury smoker's set, which included a cigarette tray, ashtray, lighter, and often, a reading lamp. The set was attached to a stand and designed to be displayed and used at home. Two decades later, simpler, portable smoking sets began to replace the larger luxury sets, as smoking became more commonplace outside the home – in restaurants, offices, and other public places.

Since their establishment during the last century, tobacconists have always attempted to emulate the conviviality of a gentlemen's private salon. Customers were invited to sample new smoking products in the shop, as most

A: Scripto gasoline and flint wheel pocket lighter with dispensing button, model H-304, by VU Light Corp., Atlanta, United States, c. 1950. Plastic and brass with chromium plating.
B: Ritepoint gasoline and flint wheel pocket lighter with dispensing button, St. Louis, United States, c. 1953. Plastic and brass with chromium plating.
C: Ritepoint gasoline and flint wheel table lighter with dispensing button, St. Louis, United States, c. 1953. Plastic and brass with chromium plating. At the top of the Scripto and the Ritepoint lighters is a small tank containing cotton wool and a wick. When the lighter was inverted and a button on its side or top was pressed, gasoline ran into the cotton wool tank.

....

A: Prince Straight-A gasoline and flint wheel pocket lighter with dispensing button, Japan, 1962. Brass with chromium plating.
B: Kaori HI-Z gasoline and flint wheel pocket lighter with dispensing button, Japan, c. 1958. Brass with chromium plating.

....

Brochure for Eldro lighters.

·············

A: Consul Druco gasoline and flint wheel table lighter with slow release system by Köllisch Brothers, Nürnberg, Germany, c. 1938. Brass with chromium plating.

B: A. P. gasoline and flint wheel table lighter with slow release system, Germany, c. 1935. Brass with chromium plating and mother-of-pearl.

C: Refill tank.

·············

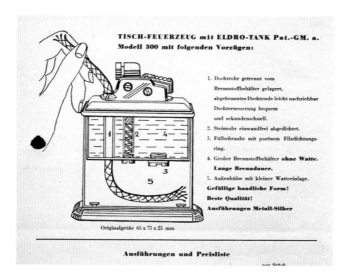

A: Eldro 200 gasoline and flint wheel pocket lighter with slow release system, Germany, c. 1950. Brass with gold plating.

B: Eldro 300 gasoline and flint wheel table lighter with slow release system, Germany, c. 1950. Brass with chromium plating; silver case.

·············

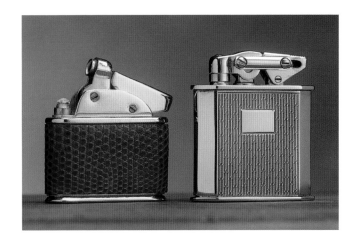

THE "DELITE" LIGHTER
(PATENT APPLIED FOR)

★ This lighter has two tanks. First remove the two screws from the bottom of the lighter and apply fuel to both tanks; one containing the wool and the other which is a reserve fuel container. There is a hole bored through the centre wall through which the fuel will slowly seep to be absorbed by the cotton wool in the other tank.

A: Luxuor gasoline and flint wheel pocket lighter with slow release system by Cauët, Paris, France, c. 1950. Brass with gold plating and leather edging.
B: Karl Wieden gasoline and flint wheel pocket lighter with slow release system, Germany, patented 1929. Brass with chromium plating.

A: Everflow gasoline and flint wheel pocket lighter with slow release system and fixed tank, United States, c. 1945. Aluminum.
B: Nu-Line gasoline and flint wheel pocket lighter with slow release system and fixed tank, United States, c. 1950. Aluminum.
C: Delite Superfine gasoline and flint wheel pocket lighter with slow release system and fixed tank, Great Britain, c. 1946. Anodized aluminum.

tobacconists had a special lighter fixed to a wall or counter that provided a constant source of flame for their smoke-loving clients. This "tobacconist's lighter" was usually connected to a central gas supply that fed methane or other manufactured gas into nearby homes or factories; it was turned on and off via a small tap operated by the customer. Later, tobacconists used more straightforward gasoline or butane gas lighters, which were placed on the counter and secured by a weight. These are still in use in contemporary tobacconists, although these stores are now more like specialty retail shops or fine delicatessens than gentlemen's studies. The traditional civility and warmth of the tobacconist, however, persists: customers are still encouraged to peruse the merchandise, ask questions, and enjoy their visit.

Coal gas

The use of gas lighters in both the home and workplace proliferated during the early twentieth century, although they were developed almost two centuries earlier, when coal gas was first discovered in Europe. A young Dutch chemistry professor named Jan Pieter Minckelers is credited with discovering the flammable properties of gas derived from coal

A: Touch-Tip classic gasoline and flint wheel table lighter by Ronson, Newark, United States, c. 1938. Metal alloy with gold plating and enamel.
B: Brown & Bigelow gasoline and flint wheel table lighter, United States, c. 1935. Brass with copper plating.
C: Gasoline and flint wheel table lighter, Austria, c. 1915. Brass with copper plating. When the pump arm of this lighter was lifted, the can containing the fuel and wick was brought to the tap; when the arm was pressed down, a spark was produced, which fell on the wick.

D: De-Light gasoline and flint wheel table lighter by Ronson, United States, patented 1928. Brass with silver plating and sharkskin.
E: Lamparina and flint wheel gasoline table lighter by Kimpel, possibly France, c. 1910. Brass with chromium plating.
F: Tresor gasoline and flint wheel table lighter by Prima Quality, model 5307, Austria, c. 1910. Brass with chromium plating.

Consul factory booklet.
....

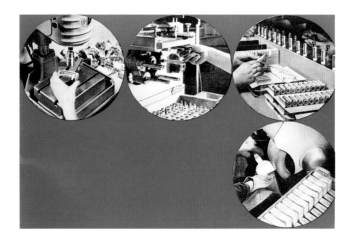

One of the earliest semi-automatic flint wheel lighters. This lighter's mechanism was reproduced by a number of different manufacturers; the most famous model was the Triplex, made by Imco of Austria.

············

A: Para-Flamme gasoline and flint wheel pocket pipe lighter by Splendid Flam, France, c. 1931. Brass with chromium plating. This model has a folding wind shield.

B: Luxuor gasoline and flint wheel pocket pipe lighter, France, c. 1930. Brass with chromium plating. In this model, the small slide on the front of the lighter pushed the tank and wick to the outside.

C: Feudor gasoline and flint wheel pocket pipe lighter, France, c. 1932. Brass with chromium plating. In this model, the entire case and wind shield can be pushed down.

A: Phillips gasoline and flint wheel pocket lighter United States, c. 1935. Brass with chromium plating and leather edging.

B: Gasoline and flint wheel semi-automatic table lighter, Austria, c. 1915. Silver with brass mechanism mounted on a wild boar's tusk. This lighter bears a hallmark that reads "G.A.S. 900" and a trademark from George Adam Scheidt, who worked in Vienna around 1900. It was probably the inspiration for the Tusk lighter made by Dunhill in 1938.

C: Derby gasoline and flint wheel pocket lighter, Germany, patented 1929. Brass with chromium plating.

D: Cyclone gasoline and flint wheel pocket lighter, Great Britain, c. 1930. Brass with chromium plating and leather edging.

E: Camlighter gasoline and flint wheel pocket lighter, Great Britain, patented 1946. Brass with chromium plating and plastic edging.

············

Banjo gasoline and flint wheel pocket lighter by Ronson, United States, c. 1926. Marked "Ronson lighter P'T'D'. December 31, 1918. Other pats P'D'S." Brass with silver plating. This was the first patented fully automatic pocket lighter with a flint wheel.

∙∙∙∙∙∙∙∙∙∙∙∙

A: Luxuor gasoline and flint wheel pocket lighter, France, c. 1931. Brass with chromium plating.
B: TCW gasoline and flint wheel pocket lighter by Treibacher Chemische Werke, Austria, c. 1935. Brass with chromium plating.
C: Bora gasoline and flint wheel pocket lighter, Austria c. 1912. Marked "M.E.B., US patent July 30, 1912." Brass with chromium plating.

∙∙∙∙∙∙∙∙∙∙∙∙

during the mid-1780s. Minckelers had been hired, along with two other scholars named Thysbaert and Van Bouchoute, by the Duke of Arensberg to investigate what kinds of gases were suitable for filling hot air balloons. Europeans had been fascinated by the hot air balloon since the Montgolfier brothers flew the first one over the rooftops of the French town of Annonay in June 1783, and innovative scientists and their patrons were eager to create more and better models. Minckelers and his colleagues were able to extract gas from straw, wool, bones, and wood, but none of these gases were light enough to float the balloon high in the air. Working on his own, Minckelers had more success when he decided to heat coal in a sealed iron tube; the gas that was produced was four times lighter than air, even when conducted through water. Minckelers also found that burning coal created an interesting by-product: a flammable gas. Because he had been experimenting with flammable materials for several years at the University of Leuven, Minckelers immediately understood the importance of his discovery – he had found a relatively simple way to make a gas that could be used as an efficient and effective fire-source. Depending on the method of extraction, means of transport, or specific purpose of this gas, it was known variously as firedamp, coke, or coal gas.

From the end of the eighteenth to the early twentieth century, public street lighting operated on coal gas, and special, remarkably long lighters were developed to facilitate the lighting of these lamps. Sometimes these long lighters were used in the home, though they were usually employed as a source of light and were not designed for use in the kitchen. Gas heat was adapted for domestic use around 1900, when gas stoves first appeared and people began to cook in much the same way they do today. At first, matches were commonly

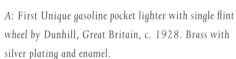

A: First Unique gasoline pocket lighter with single flint wheel by Dunhill, Great Britain, c. 1928. Brass with silver plating and enamel.

B: Zippo gasoline and flint wheel pocket lighter, United States, c. 1932. Brass with chromium plating. This was the first model Zippo made with a hinge on the outside of the lighter.

C: Beney gasoline and flint wheel pocket lighter, model 202, Great Britain, c. 1935. Brass and leather with chromium plating. This early Beney model featured an unusual spring system for the lift arm.

A: The White gasoline and flint wheel pocket lighter, United States, c. 1930. Brass with chromium plating.

B: The Light House gasoline and flint wheel pocket lighter, patented in Germany, c. 1930. Brass with chromium plating.

C: Electrik gasoline and flint wheel semi-rotating pocket lighter, Germany, c. 1920. Brass with chromium plating.

Colibri "Original" gasoline and flint wheel pocket lighter, Switzerland, c. 1928. Brass with chromium plating. This was the first Colibri model to feature an open spring mechanism.

....

A: King gasoline and flint wheel table lighter by Pino, Austria, c. 1930. Brass with chromium plating.
B: Gasoline and flint wheel table lighter, Austria, c. 1915. Brass with chromium plating.
C: Thorens gasoline and flint wheel table lighter, model 700, Switzerland, c. 1920. Marked "USA pat. 3 Feb., 1914, British pat. Jan. 29, 1920." Brass with chromium plating.

....

used to light gas stoves, but soon, the newer pocket and table lighters became popular in the kitchen. Stove lighters that were connected to a central electric supply or that ran on batteries, as well as flint-wheel stove lighters, were also introduced. Flint-wheel lighters were used outside the home by welders, laboratory technicians, and glassblowers, all of whom wanted a quick and safe way to light their implements.

The development of fuel containers

Along with gas, alcohol, methanol, and gasoline have been the primary sources of fuel for lighters over the centuries. Lighters that use liquid fuels, such as alcohol and gasoline, had to be designed with a storage system for the fuel. At first, porous materials such as cotton wool were used, but the storage capacity of such products is very limited; special tanks had to be designed in order to store more gasoline. Eventually, four different types of tanks for lighters were developed, all designed with an eye toward increasing fuel storage capacity.

The cotton wool tank lighter combines a wick with a cotton wool tank. The wick protrudes from the container with cotton wool and is drenched with fuel; the gasoline-soaked wick is then ignited. These lighters were made either with or without a separate tank, and could be refilled with gasoline via an opening underneath, above, or on the side of the lighter.

Lighters that work on a "slow release system" combine a cotton wool tank and a gasoline container. The filling screw on this double-compartment tank has a small opening for a wick or a piece of felt to go around the screw (or both a wick and a piece of felt) through which the gasoline slowly seeps into the

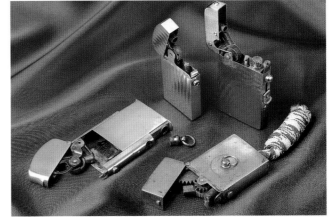

A: Gasoline and flint wheel table lighter, France, c. 1935. Brass with chromium plating and plastic edging.
B: Gasoline and flint wheel table lighter, France c. 1935. Brass with chromium plating and leather edging; silver emblem.
C: M.E.B. gasoline and flint wheel table lighter, France, c. 1938. Brass with chromium plating.
D: G. D. gasoline and flint wheel table lighter, France, c. 1915. Marked "Allumette Metallique Eternelle." Brass with chromium plating.
E: Karl Wieden gasoline and flint wheel table lighter, Germany, c. 1935. Brass with chromium plating and celluloid edging.
....

A: Chronos gasoline and flint wheel pocket lighter, model G, Austria, c. 1913. Brass with chromium plating.
B: W & P gasoline and flint wheel pocket lighter, Germany, c. 1915. Brass with chromium plating.
C: E. D. gasoline and semi-rotating flint wheel pocket lighter by Emil Deutsch, Vienna, c. 1911. Marked "D.R.G.M. ges.gesch., REGD. No. 573341. DEPOSE, S176, patent 1911." Brass with chromium plating.

A: Gasoline and flint wheel pocket lighter, Austria, c. 1910. Silver, brass, and steel. B: Gasoline and flint wheel pocket lighter, possibly Germany, c. 1920. Brass with chromium plating. This lighter inlcudes a safety catch.

C: Record gasoline and flint wheel pocket lighter, Austria, c. 1911. Brass with chromium plating. Imprinted with a French tax seal.
D: Fusee and flint wheel pocket lighter, Germany, c. 1910. Brass with chromium plating.
In early semi-automatic lighters such as these, a lid closed off the wick; all of them had a rotating flint wheel, except for the second from left, which had a semi-rotating flint wheel. A spring in the cover was often used to press against the flint, although some versions of these lighters inlcuded a separate spring for this particular function. Gasoline, a fusee, or a combination of the two, were used as fuel.
....

Right: *A: Thorens gasoline and flint wheel pocket lighter, Switzerland, c. 1920. Marked "Thorens, Swiss made, USA pat. Feb. 3, 1914/Nov. 16, 1920, Thorens Inc., New York." Brass, nickel, and silver with leather edging. This was the first Thorens semi-automatic lighter; it was distinctive because of its flint wheel, which was a separately fitted component.*
B: Erlac gasoline and flint wheel pocket lighter, France, c. 1940. Brass with silver plating. This lighter, which featured a semi-automatic cover, was also produced under the Dunhill name.
C: Everest gasoline and flint wheel pocket lighter, Switzerland, c. 1930. Brass with silver plating and sharkskin.

Below: A: Super gasoline and flint wheel pocket lighter by Imco, Austria, c. 1929. Brass. The flint mechanism in this lighter is the same as that in a pipe lighter; a separate leaf spring was included to keep the snuffer open, which had to be closed manually.
B: Imco 2000 gasoline and flint wheel pocket lighter, Austria, c. 1929. Brass. In this model, both the snuffer and the wind shield were operated by hand.

C: Jimco gasoline and flint wheel pocket lighter, Austria, c. 1920. Marked "M.E.B., J. Meister & Co., Vienna." Brass. This was the first model in Imco's range that did not feature a wind shield; the snuffer had to be both opened and closed manually.
D: Föhn gasoline and flint wheel pocket lighter by Imco, Austria, c. 1926. Brass.
E: Ifa gasoline and flint wheel pocket lighter by Imco, Austria, c. 1927. Brass. In this model, the snuffer is connected by a bracket to the tank; it opened automatically when the wind shield was pushed up, and closed when the operation was reversed.
F: Ifa 440 gasoline and flint wheel pocket lighter by Imco, Austria, c. 1936. Brass. This is a modified version of the earlier Ifa.
G: Imco 2200 gasoline and flint wheel pocket pipe lighter, Austria, c. 1930. Brass. This model was designed to be a pipe lighter; the tank and burner could be separated from the rest of the lighter mechanism in order to properly light a pipe.

A: E.P.H. gasoline and flint wheel table lighter, possibly Austria, c. 1920. Brass with chromium plating.

B: E.P.H. gasoline and flint wheel table lighter, model 392, possibly Austria, c. 1920. Brass with chromium plating. In order to ignite this lighter, the arm and the flint wheel had to be brought close to the wick.

C: Champion gasoline and flint wheel pocket lighter, Germany, c. 1920. Brass with chromium plating.

D: Admira gasoline and flint wheel pocket lighter, Austria, c. 1920. Brass with chromium plating and aluminum mirror.

E: A. D. gasoline and flint wheel pocket lighter, Austria, c. 1930. Brass with chromium plating.

Gasoline and flint wheel signet ring lighter, Germany, c. 1935. Brass.

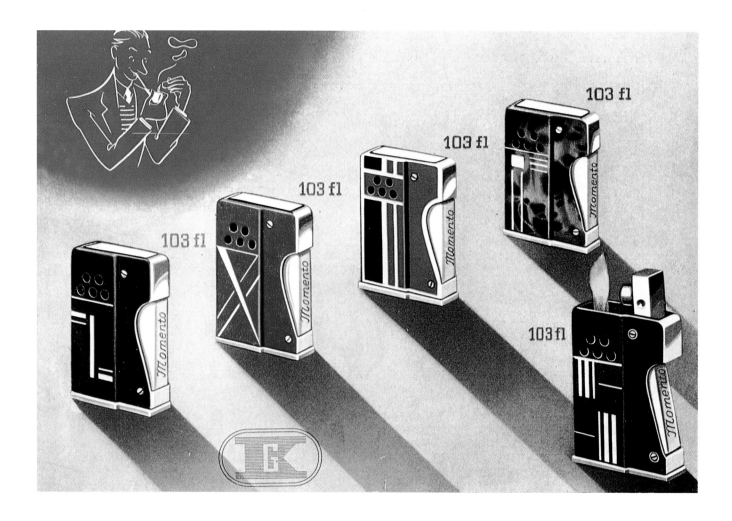

Brochure for Consul pocket lighters.

Ever Light gasoline and flint wheel pocket lighter, Germany, patented 1929. Brass with chromium plating. The gears in this lighter allowed the flint wheel to rotate very rapidly, producing a great shower of sparks.

············

Deniel's gasoline and flint wheel table lighter, France,
c. 1935. Brass with chromium plating.

• • • • • • • • • • • •

A: McMurdo gasoline and flint wheel table lighter,
Great Britain, c. 1950. Brass wih chromium plating.
B: Three McMurdo gasoline and flint wheel pocket
lighters, Great Britain, c. 1950. Brass with
chromium plating.

Lord gasoline and flint wheel pocket lighter, Germany,
c. 1930. Brass with chromium plating. This model
opens when the lower sides of the lighter are pressed.

• • • • • • • • • • •

cotton wool container. A patent for this model was granted to the German firm of KW in 1930, although its director, Karl Wieden, had already patented a similar, earlier version in 1915. The appeal of the slow release system lighter is its efficient combination of an absorbent cotton wool tank with the greater storage capacity of a liquid gasoline container. The filling screw connects the two compartments, and the fuel is dispensed via a piece of felt or a hole with a fusee (or sometimes both), which allows for controlled seepage of the gasoline. Because the filling screw cannot be reached from the outside, the lighter must be refilled by lifting the whole tank out.

The dispenser system lighter also combines a liquid and a cotton wool tank. The dispenser is on the liquid gasoline compartment; by pressing a button, gasoline is added to the cotton wool between the two tanks. As the fuel-soaked material burns, the lighter's flame become less intense, indicating that more gasoline must be added to the cotton wool.

Yet another type of lighter that operates on the slow release system uses separate, self-contained tanks for the gasoline and the cotton wool. The fuel is transported through a tube that links the two tanks. The transfer of gasoline is controlled by the position of the tube: both ends of the tube meet the screw threads from the filling caps of each tank, so that the fuel seeps at a slow pace into the cotton wool – in much the same way that the gasoline drips through a piece of felt in the original slow release system lighter. The two tanks

A: Glamalita gasoline and flint wheel pocket lighter and pencil, Great Britain, c. 1930. Brass with gold plating.

B: Tempo gasoline and flint wheel pocket lighter and propeller pencil, France, c. 1930. Bakelite. This lighter includes a storage space for pencil leads.

••••••••••••

A: Stewart gasoline and flint wheel pocket lighter and propeller pencil, United States, c. 1932. Brass with gold plating.

B: Stewart gasoline and flint wheel pocket lighter and propeller pencil, United States, c. 1935. Brass with gold plating. Both of these Stewart lighters have storage spaces for extra cartridges.

C: Havalite gasoline and flint wheel pocket lighter and propeller pencil, United States, c. 1935. Bakelite and brass with chromium plating.

D: Penciliter gasoline and flint wheel pocket lighter and propeller pencil by Ronson, United States, patented 1947. Brass, rhodium plate. Like the preceding Havalite, this lighter includes storage space for cartridges and erasers.

E: Gasoline and flint wheel pocket lighter and propeller pencil, Austria, patented 1941. Brass with chromium plating and plastic.

F: Gasoline and flint wheel pocket lighter and propeller pencil, Austria, patented 1941. Brass with silver plating and plastic.

••••••••••••

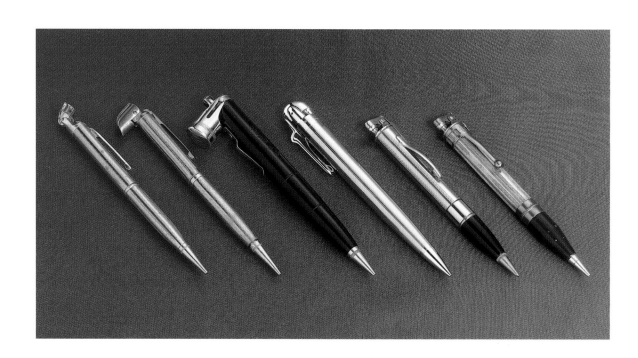

A: Clip 2850 gas and flint wheel pocket lighter by Consul, Germany, c. 1968. Brass with gold plating and lacquer. This model was produced by Diplomat / Birwill of Switzerland.
B: J.J.J. Carol gas and flint wheel pocket lighter, c. 1980. Brass with chromium plating.
C: Clip-on gas and flint wheel pocket lighter, Japan, c. 1982. Anodized aluminum and brass with chromium plating.
D: Gas and flint wheel pocket lighter, Japan, c. 1979. Anodized aluminum and brass with chromium plating.
E: Hadson gas and flint wheel pocket lighter, Japan, c. 1978. Plastic, brass aluminum with chromium plating and anodized.

. . . .

A: Esterd gas and flint wheel pocket lighter, model 19, by Kawasaki Seiko, Tokyo, Japan, 1978. Brass and steel with gold plating and plastic screw top. In this lighter, the burner opens when a button is pushed and the flint wheel appears. When the button is pressed again, the flint wheel automatically disappears into the case and the burner shuts off.
B: Cliplite gas and flint wheel pocket pipe lighter by Maxim, the Netherlands, c. 1979. Brass with gold plating.
C: Idalite gasoline and flint wheel pocket lighter by Elgin, United States, c. 1950. Brass with chromium plating.
D: Colibri gas with piezo ignition pocket lighter, Great Britain, c. 1978. Lacquered brass with gold plating. This design features a dual cover: when swivelled in one direction it exposes the burner, and when turned the opposite way it reveals the filler valve. Produced for Colibri by the Crown Company of Japan, this model was never actually marketed.
E: Colibri gas and flint wheel pocket pipe lighter, Great Britain, c. 1979. Brass with chromium plating and lacquer.

. . . .

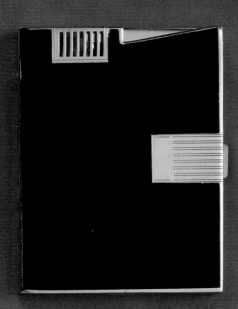

function like permanent lighter components and do not have to be replaced; the filling screws can be reached from the outside when refills are necessary.

The lighter during wartime

During both the First and Second World Wars, metal household goods such as lighters became available only on a limited scale, as manufacturing efforts – particularly within the steel industry – were almost solely directed toward producing arms and other war supplies. Because smoking remained immensely popular during these tumultuous times, people began creating various homemade lighters; the unique conditions of war spawned a variety of inventive models. The "trench-art" lighter, named after the infamous deep ditches dug in Europe during World War I, was made from bullets, helmets, coins, and buttons, and appears to have been put together by soldiers struggling at the front lines. The image of a soldier who is surrounded by heavy fighting having the leisure to create a lighter from parts of his uniform, however, seems very romantic and highly improbable. It is far more likely that trench-art lighters were made by civilians living close to the front lines who gathered remnants of the belongings soldiers left behind, then constructed the lighters and traded them with the soldiers for food, clothing, or cigarettes.

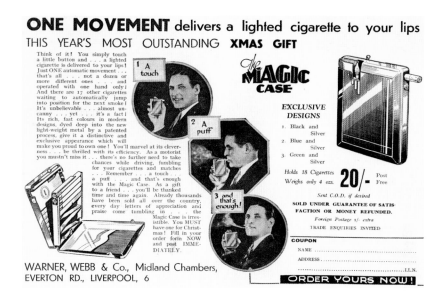

A: Patrician gasoline and flint wheel pocket lighter with cigarette case by Ronson, United States, c. 1939. Brass with chromium plating and enamel.

B: Gasoline and flint wheel pocket lighter with cigarette case, Japan, c. 1960. Brass with chromium plating and enamel.

C: Light-o-matic Magic Action gasoline and flint wheel pocket lighter with cigarette case by Elgin, United States, c. 1955. Brass with gold plating.

D: Moon-light gasoline and flint wheel pocket lighter with cigarette case by Pearl, Japan, c. 1955. Brass with chromium plating and Perspex.

E: Gasoline and flint wheel pocket lighter with cigarette case, Great Britain, c. 1935. Brass with chromium plating.

F: Hadson gasoline and flint wheel pocket lighter with cigarette case, Japan, c. 1952. Brass with chromium plating and Perspex. The interior of the lighter is engraved in Dutch: "To Mr. A. N. Liefveld, a souvenir of Ong Tiong, Solo, September 5, 1952."

G: Reform gasoline and flint wheel pocket lighter with cigarette case, Austria, c. 1947. Steel with chromium plating.

H: Superpact gasoline and flint wheel pocket lighter with cigarette case and compact by Ronson, United States, c. 1933. Brass with gold plating and enamel.

· · · · · · · · · · · ·

Advertisement for The Magic Case cigarette holder and lighter, "The Illustrated London News," December 1, 1934.

A: Franklin gasoline and flint wheel pocket lighter with cigarette case, model 54, United States, c. 1954. Lacquered aluminum.

B: Razzia gasoline and flint wheel pocket lighter with cigarette case, Germany, c. 1955. Bakelite and brass with chromium plating.

· · · · · · · · · · · ·

A: *Gasoline and flint wheel table lighter, Great Britain,*
c. 1920. Brass with leather edging; wooden base.

B: *Gasoline and flint wheel table lighter, France,*
c. 1915. Brass and copper.

C: *Gasoline and flint wheel table lighter, Great Britain,*
c. 1945. Marked with the royal coat of arms and
inscribed "Coronation of George V, June 1911." Brass.

D: *Gasoline and flint wheel pocket lighter, possibly*
France, c. 1915. Brass.

E: *Gasoline and flint wheel table lighter, possibly*
Germany, c. 1915. Brass.

· · · · · · · · · · ·

Trench-art lighters have remained extremely popular, partially due to the aura of romance and heroism imparted by the legendary image of the soldier laboring over a lighter in the cold ditches of war-torn Europe. Today, trench-art lighters are highly sought-after collectors' items that sell for hundreds of dollars. Because they are so valuable, trench-art lighters have been widely copied; there are now a number of fakes on the market. Not every maker of imitation trench-art lighters, however, is ill-intentioned. An American named Thomas Prilinski creates delightful replicas with coins that look deceptively old, though he signs all his work "Pyro;" and a well-known collector named Jean Bernard brought ninety homemade trench-art lighters to the 1991 International Collectors' Fair in Villerest, France, all of which he had assembled in his spare time.

Utility lighters

Matches were especially scarce in Britain during World War II – when the island-nation was cut off from mainland Europe – and demand for lighters skyrocketed. The metal required to produce lighters, however, was needed by the munitions industry, and the government imposed strict regulations on lighter manufacturers. In Britain in 1941, a mechanical lighter could contain no more than three-quarters of an ounce of brass, had to be marked "UL" (for "utility lighter"), and could cost no more than five shillings (about a dollar). The export of lighters to the European continent came to a standstill; lighter manufacturers such as Dunhill, Polo, Benlow, Colibri, and Beney stayed in business by making these simpler, less profitable utility lighters and by selling wicks, flints, and lighter fuel. The British government also set prices for these individual lighter supplies.

Alfred Dunhill managed to circumvent some of these restrictions for a while because of his relationship with the Swiss firm La Nationale, a company that had been producing lighters for Dunhill since before World War II. During the war,

Five gasoline and flint wheel pocket lighters, France, c. 1915. Various combinations of brass, copper, and silver.

A: Eley gasoline and flint wheel pocket lighter, Great Britain, c. 1915. Brass and copper.

B: Gasoline and flint wheel pocket lighter, possibly Great Britain, c. 1945. Brass.

C: Gasoline and flint wheel pocket lighter, Germany, c. 1915. Brass.

A: Gasoline and flint wheel pocket lighter, France, c. 1918. Brass and bronze. On the front of the lighter is a British penny dated 1917; on the reverse is a French ten-centimes coin dated 1907.

B: Gasoline and flint wheel pocket lighter, possibly Italy, c. 1915. Brass and nickel. Italian twenty-centecimi coins, dated 1911, adorn both the front and back of this lighter.

A: Pyro gasoline and flint wheel pocket lighter, United States, 1991. Brass. This lighter, which features a commemorative Dutch two-and-a-half guilder coin dated 1979, was made especially for the Dutch Lighter Museum by collector and lighter-maker Thomas Prylinski.

B: Gasoline and flint wheel pocket lighter, France, c. 1945. Brass and bronze. This is a factory-made version of the trench-art lighters that were first created and popularized during World War I. The lighter is made in several different sizes.

•••••••••••

A: *Gasoline and flint wheel table lighter,*
Great Britain, c. 1945. Brass with wooden foot.
B: *Gasoline and flint wheel table lighter, Great*
Britain, c. 1945. Brass with chromium plating.
The base of this lighter contains a filling screw made
from an English three-penny coin dated 1940.
C: *The Matt Lighter gasoline and flint wheel pocket*
lighter, model V3, Great Britain, c. 1912. Brass
with silver plating.
D: *Gasoline and flint wheel pocket lighter, Austria,*
c. 1945. Galvanized steel.
E: *Gasoline and flint wheel table lighter, Germany,*
c. 1945. Brass.
F: *Gasoline and flint wheel pocket lighter, Germany,*
c. 1920. Steel with chromium plating.

•••••••••••

La Nationale made and supplied lighters directly to Dunhill customers in mainland Europe. However, La Nationale's production did eventually suffer because of the widespread shortage of metals normally used to make lighters – in 1943, Dunhill's brand name lighter was made from a zinc alloy. It is worth noting that the war shortages were beneficial to one model, the catalytic lighter, which does not require gasoline and is made with only a small amount of metal.

Since the arms industry laid claim to most supplies of copper, brass, and steel, lighter producers had to look for other usable manufacturing materials. Aluminum from shot-down aircraft, which was sold as scrap metal, was used for lighter casings; steel was reserved for the moveable parts and hinges. The processing of this scrap aluminum required special methods and machines. Usually, the aluminum was cast into a block, which was then hollowed out to create space for the steel or brass hinges, the fuel tank, and the flint mechanism. The development of this new manufacturing technique became a valuable investment for lighter companies, as the aluminum lighter remained a profitable

product until the 1970s. After the war, manufacturers began to anodize the aluminum so that the lighters could be made in different colors – and would not be permanently associated with the privations of wartime. The process of anodizing by electrodeposition gave the aluminum casing a thick, protective oxide coating that both prevented corrosion and embellished the lighter.

During the 1950s and 1960s, aluminum lighters that incorporated additional materials such as brass, Perspex, and various other plastics appeared on the market. By the 1970s, the production of aluminum lighters requiring traditional hollowing and cutting methods began to decline, largely due to the development of new, more efficient molding and casting techniques. These newer methods were particularly well suited to the manufacture of plastic lighter components, which soon surpassed the production of aluminum alloy models. Moreover, it was soon discovered that the manufacture of aluminum lighters threatened the environment: extracting aluminum from bauxite consumes vast amounts of energy and is not an environment-friendly process.

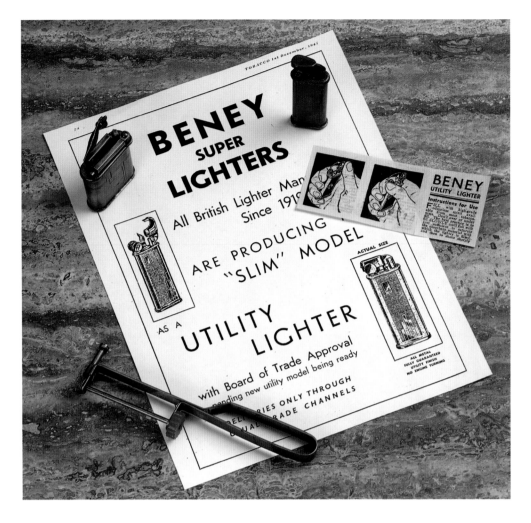

A: "UL Popular" gasoline and flint wheel utility pocket lighter by Beney, Great Britain, c. 1943. Anodized steel.

B: Beney gasoline and flint wheel utility pocket lighter, Great Britain, c. 1941. Anodized steel.

C: Lytup flint wheel utility stove lighter, Great Britain, c. 1942. Anodized steel.

Utility lighters featured in "Tobacco" magazine, December 1, 1941.

....

A: Benlow gasoline and flint wheel utility pocket lighter, Great Britain, c. 1943. Lacquered steel. B: Three Wheel gasoline and flint wheel utility pocket lighter by Benlow, Great Britain, c. 1944. Steel and lacquered enamel.

C: Autoflik gasoline and flint wheel utility pocket lighter by Colibri, Great Britain, c. 1945. Aluminum and steel with chromium plating. D: Polo gasoline and flint wheel utility pocket lighter, Great Britain, c. 1942. Plastic and brass. E: Polo gasoline and flint wheel utility pocket lighter, Great Britain, c. 1942. Steel with chromium plating.

....

A: *Dicast gasoline and flint wheel utility pocket lighter by Ora, Great Britain, c. 1945. Metal alloy and lacquered enamel.*

B: *Wunup gasoline and flint wheel utililty pocket lighter, Great Britain, c. 1946. Lacquered steel.*

C: *Ebil gasoline and flint wheel utility pocket lighter, Great Britain, c. 1944. Bakelite and steel.*

••••••••••••

A: *The Rosedale gasoline and flint striker utility pocket lighter, Great Britain, c. 1944. Plastic.*

B: *Victory gasoline and flint wheel lighter, Great Britain, c. 1946. Brass with chromium plating.*

••••••••••••

The cult of the new

Although the great war effort of the 1930s and 1940s dominated industrial production in Europe and the United States, another powerful movement was beginning that was to permanently alter the global marketplace: the age of advertising and mass consumption. For the first time in history, manufacturers, designers, and advertisers were joining forces to both meet the demands of their customers and to cultivate the public's desire for new, better, and always, more products. Everyday commodities were redesigned and relaunched on an annual basis; new car models began to appear every autumn, and household appliances quickly became obsolete as engineers and designers added novel features to their newest models. The aesthetic and material gratification of the cult of the new would eventually extract a heavy toll on society, particularly in the United States, where production and consumption of energy and goods reached – and remain today – at world-record levels. As German designer Dieter Rams, who pioneered the Braun company's dedication to functional minimalism observed, the effects of mass consumption are both physical and visual pollution: there are too many products and too many designs glutting the marketplace.

When the design mania of the twentieth century first began, however, the atmosphere of competitive innovation presented an unprecedented challenge to designers and manufacturers working in every field, including the lighter and smoking industries. Large numbers of graphic artists, illustrators, and painters, as well as industrial designers, were lured into the world of big business and advertising.

The legendary American designer Raymond Loewy achieved great success with his reworking of the logo for Lucky Strike cigarettes – a design Loewy himself considered one of his very best. This project was actually the result of a bet between the designer and the chief executive of the American Tobacco Company, George Washington Hill. The year was 1940, and Lucky Strike was one of the most popular cigarette brands of the day, with yearly sales approaching 1,000,000. The packaging for Lucky Strike had remained unchanged since its original design in 1917, and the American Tobacco Company saw little room for improvement. Loewy, however, was convinced that it was time for a change, and he bet Hill $50,000 that he could produce a new design that would significantly increase the brand's revenue. Apparently, shortly after Loewy arrived home from this meeting, a carton of Lucky Strikes was delivered with a card that read, "Shove these under your pillow; sweet dreams." Two weeks later Loewy returned the carton with a new design: the original green of the packaging had been changed to white, so that the target in the center of the pack, bearing the brand name, stood out much more clearly. Loewy also put the target motif and brand name on both sides of the cigarette pack, giving consumers two opportunities, rather than one, to read and remember the name. Moreover, Loewy had perhaps unwittingly resolved a problem formerly presented by using so much green ink; the ink smelled and had to be neutralized in order to prevent contaminating the cigarettes. With the new, predominantly white packaging that featured the brand name and logo on both sides of the packet, Lucky Strike's profits rose by seventeen percent. Loewy had won his bet.

The legend of the Zippo lighter

While many industrial manufacturers were eager to churn out new products and designs every year to satiate the public's thirst for novelty, some of the most successful manufacturers pursued a policy of quality and longevity, effectively rejecting the tenets of "throw-away" consumerism. One of these was the Zippo Manufacturing Company, founded by inventor George Grant Blaisdell in Bradford, Pennsylvania. The design for the famous Zippo lighter has remained unchanged since it first appeared on the market in 1932. Blaisdell's lighter was really a redesign of a simple Austrian model that was efficient but awkward to use. The Austrian inventor apparently had no interest in perfecting his design, so Blaisdell adapted and improved it, with great results. Blaisdell put the original body into a simple brass casing, protected the wick with a larger shield to make it windproof, and added a large, serrated wheel, which was easy to operate and guaranteed a good ignition. Blaisdell called his new lighter the Zippo – a short, catchy, and very memorable name.

A: Gasoline and flint wheel pocket lighter, Germany. Inscribed in Dutch: "From Louis, from Mac, for Bert Sieburg, 17-2-44." Aluminum and lacquer.
B: Gasoline and flint wheel pocket lighter, France, c. 1945. Aluminum and brass.

A: Gasoline and flint wheel pocket lighter, United States, c. 1950. Marked "F.F.J." Aluminum and Perspex. The protruding section on the front of the lighter is a compartment for spare flints.
B: Gasoline and flint wheel pocket lighter, United States, c. 1945. Aluminum with inlaid plastic stripes.
C: Wagner Deluxe gasoline and flint wheel pocket lighter, United States, c. 1950. Aluminum.

A: Gasoline and flint wheel table lighter, Great Britain, c. 1948. Aluminum with plastic foot.

B: Gasoline and flint wheel table lighter, France, c. 1945. Aluminum and brass with chromium-plated lid. The upper part of the ball had to be unscrewed when the lighter needed to be filled.

C: New Yorker gasoline and flint wheel table lighter, United States, c. 1955. Lacquered aluminum. The base of this lighter contains a compartment for spare flints and the filling screw includes a tool for changing the flint.

D: Hand-built gasoline and flint wheel table lighter, Great Britain, c. 1950. Aluminum.

E: Dupont gasoline and flint wheel pocket lighter, France, c. 1942. Aluminum and brass with gold-plated mechanism. This was Dupont's utility- lighter model.

F: Schnaben gasoline and flint wheel pocket lighter, Germany, c. 1945. Aluminum and lacquered enamel. In order to fill this unique lighter, the top had to be unscrewed and the base removed.

G: Feudor 100 gasoline and flint wheel pocket lighter, France, c. 1944. Aluminum. This is the utility-lighter version of the Feudor 100.

•••••••••••

The Zippo was an overnight success. It was very popular in the American armed forces, as this reliable lighter developed a masculine image that appealed to the soldiers, and, moreover, the Zippo provided a powerful reminder of home. During World War II, the Korean War, and the Vietnam War, American soldiers engraved their names, birth dates, and even their wills on Zippo lighters, many of which were left behind on the battlefront. Today, these souvenirs of war are as highly sought-after by collectors as the trench-art lighters of World War I, and equally as prone to imitation. Visitors to the battlefields of southeast Asia are now presented with Zippo lighters, often complete with emotional inscriptions – messages scribbled only hours earlier by the proprietor of the local tourist trade.

Along with its historical associations, today's Zippo remains the world's best-selling instant lighter. Its simple design and efficient technology have made the Zippo a truly timeless product, with a lifetime guarantee.

A: Tops gasoline and flint wheel pocket lighter, United States, c. 1945. Aluminum.
B: Gasoline and flint wheel pocket lighter, France, c. 1950. Marked "Déposé." Aluminum.
C: Savent gasoline and flint wheel pocket lighter, France, c. 1945. Marked "Marque déposé, Bté, SGDG-PV. 490019." Aluminum.

A: Rollalite gasoline and flint wheel pocket lighter by Dunhill, made by La Nationale, Geneva, c. 1943. Zinc. This was Dunhill's utility-lighter model.
B: Crown gasoline and flint wheel pocket lighter, United States, c. 1948. Aluminum.
C: Sharpo gasoline and flint wheel pocket lighter, United States, c. 1945. Aluminum.

············

A: Gasoline and flint wheel table lighter, possibly the
Netherlands, c. 1948. Aluminum and brass with
chromium-plated foot; enamel shields on front and
back.
B: Gasoline and flint wheel table lighter, Great Britain,
c. 1950. Anodized aluminum.
C: Pahaa gasoline and flint wheel table lighter, Great
Britain, c. 1946. Aluminum.

A: Duchess gasoline and flint wheel pocket lighter by
Flamidor, France, c. 1947. Anodized aluminum.
B: Gasoline and flint wheel pocket lighter, Great
Britain, c. 1947. Aluminum.
C: Golmet gasoline and flint wheel pocket lighter by
Benlow, Great Britain, c. 1946. Anodized aluminum.

....

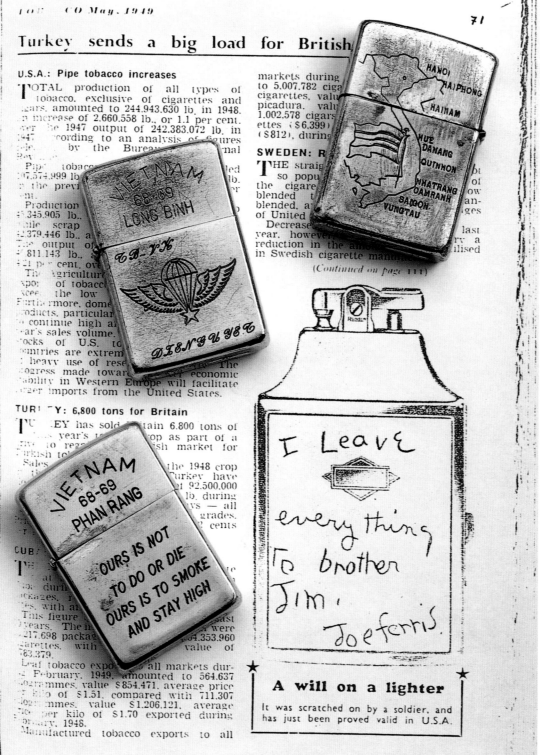

Three Regular gasoline and flint wheel pocket lighters
by Zippo, United States, c. 1967–68. Brass with
chromium plating.

············

A: Original gasoline and flint wheel pocket lighter by
Karl Wieden, Germany, c. 1935. Brass with
chromium plating.
B: Drago gasoline and flint wheel pocket lighter marked
Insignes Militaires, France, c. 1950. Brass with silver
plating.

A: Regular gasoline and flint wheel pocket lighter by
Zippo, United States, 1994. Brass and lacquered
enamel.
B: Regular gasoline and flint wheel pocket lighter by
Zippo, United States, 1945. Steel and lacquered
enamel.

....

Made in France
Quercia
Brevets France et Etranger

Postwar Revolution

A: Gentry gas and flint wheel table lighter by Flaminaire, France, 1947. Brass with gold plating an lacquer. This was the first butane gas lighter sold.
B: Gentry gas and flint wheel table lighter by Flaminaire, France, 1947. Brass with silver plating.
C: Grillon gas and flint wheel pocket lighter by Flaminaire, France, 1948. Brass with chromium plating. This was the first gas pocket lighter made by Flaminaire. In the foreground is the refill tank, for the gentry.

A: Karl Wieden gasoline and flint wheel pocket lighter, model 1261/310S, Germany, c. 1950. Brass with chromium plating and lacquer.
B: Karl Wieden gas and flint wheel pocket lighter, Germany, possibly c. 1950. Brass with chromium plating. This gas prototype lighter is from KW's 1200 range, probably produced after World War II.
C: Karl Wieden gas and flint wheel pocket lighter, Germany, c. 1939. Brass with chromium plating. Launched at the Leipzig trade fair in 1939, this was the first butane gas lighter ever presented to the world. Largely due to the outbreak of World War II, it never went into production.
D: Dorgento 850 gasoline and flint wheel pocket lighter by Karl Wieden, Germany, patented 1930. Brass with chromium plating; silver case.

•••••••••••

The violence of war and the hardship of economic instability that rocked the globe during the 1930s and 1940s affected every sector of society, temporarily curtailing the flood of invention that had swept across the industrialized world in the early part of the century.

A: Galet gas and flint wheel pocket lighter by
Flaminaire, France, 1959. Aluminum and brass with
lacquer and gold plating.
B: Galaxi gas and flint wheel table lighter by
Flaminaire, France, 1962. Brass with chromium
plating.

A: Karl Wieden gas and flint wheel table lighter,
Germany, possibly c. 1950. Brass with chromium
plating. On this model, the gas tank is separate.
B: Karl Wieden gasoline and flint wheel table lighter,
model 6760, Germany, patented 1930. Brass with
chromium plating.
C: Original 135 gasoline and flint wheel pocket lighter
by Karl Wieden, Germany, c. 1937. Brass with
chromium plating.
D: Original gas and flint wheel pocket lighter by Karl
Wieden, Germany, c. 1955. Brass with chromium
plating.

....

When the butane gas lighter was first introduced, a
number of manufacturers began simply converting
their existing gasoline lighters into gas models. This method allowed
producers both to save money and to quickly meet the demands of their
customers.

....

A: Monopol gasoline and flint wheel pocket lighter by Colibri,
Great Britain, 1934. Brass with chromium plating.
B: Gaz-small gas and flint wheel pocket lighter by Colibri,
France, 1955. Brass with chromium plating.
C: Triplex gasoline and flint wheel pocket lighter by Imco,
Austria, c. 1937. Steel with chromium plating.
D: G11 gas and flint wheel pocket lighter by Imco, Austria,
c. 1964. Aluminum and plastic with gold plating.

•••••••••••

A: Diplomat gas and flint wheel table lighter by
Mylflam, Germany, c. 1960. Brass with chromium
plating; silver-plated case.
B: "Mylflam", Diplomat, Germany, c. 1950. Petrol.
Brass, chromium plated.

•••••••••••

The New York stock market crash of 1929 ushered in an era of
bankruptcy and poverty that spread across the United States
and was not arrested until President Franklin Delano
Roosevelt's New Deal program – and shortly thereafter, World
War II – put Americans back to work. In Europe, high inflation
and unemployment fermented the political unrest in Germany
that preceded the devastating rise of Nazism in the late 1930s.
The growth of fascism in Italy and Japan, and of Stalin's
despotic consolidation of power in the new Soviet Union,
brought war and privation to the rest of Europe, Asia, and parts
of Africa. It was not until the war finally ended in 1945 that
people could concentrate on much more than survival at home
and victory on the battlefront.

Like every other industry not directly associated with the
war effort, the lighter trade suffered from a scarcity of
resources during this period. Inspired inventors and
determined manufacturers continued to research and make
significant discoveries in the field, but relatively few new
models were designed, and still fewer patent applications were
submitted. Often, a patent for an invention was filed "on hold"

for a future date, as manufacturers hesitated to invest in a new product when money and materials were hard to come by, and were usually needed for the war effort. One of the most important advances in the history of the lighter, the gas lighter, was invented (and actually patented) in the mid-1930s, but was not fully developed or produced until after the war. By this time, there were several ambitious lighter manufacturers who were eager to make and market this new innovation.

The butane gas lighter

The origins of the butane gas lighter date back to 1933, when Otto Reich and Julius Vignati of Vienna patented their burner for a lighter that ran on carbide gas. Reich and Vignati were known to have patented a number of products for the German Karl Wieden (KW) company during the 1930s, and it is safe to assume that their innovative lighter burner was among them – though no clear documentation of this transaction has been found. In any case, nothing was heard of the new burner until 1939, when KW introduced the first butane gas lighter to the public at the Leipzig trade fair. Because the German war machine was gaining tremendous momentum at this time, there were almost no industrial resources available for the development of commercial products such as this new lighter. After the war, production and promotion of non-essential goods had to wait until reconstruction was largely over. Though the US-led Marshall plan helped to rebuild West Germany fairly quickly – a phenomenon referred to as a Wirtschaftswunder (a period of remarkable economic recovery) by many Germans living in this Allied-protected region – the German lighter industry lost the pioneering lead it might have claimed had the Third Reich not applied all the nation's resources to war.

Reich and Vignati's innovation was quickly followed by a similar gas lighter patented by a Frenchman named Henri Pingeot in 1935. Pingeot, a manufacturer of safety valves for tires, was a fervent patriot who firmly believed that a French invention must remain within the country's borders, and hence he dismissed all foreign applications to adopt his design. Instead, Pingeot began searching for a suitable partner to produce his gas lighter in France. Pingeot settled on the well

A: *Verona gas and flint wheel table lighter by Ronson, United States, c. 1950. Brass with silver plating. This was Ronson's first gas table lighter made with a detachable, refillable tank.*
B: *Vanguard gas and flint wheel pocket lighter by Ronson, United States, c. 1950. Brass with chromium plating and enamel.*
C: *Whirlwind gasoline and flint wheel pocket lighter by Ronson, Great Britain, c. 1946. Brass with chromium plating and leather edging.*

Slide automatic gas and petrol and flint wheel table lighters both by Hilton, possibly Japan, c. 1955. Brass with chromium plating and leather and plastic stand; brass with chromium plating and plastic foot.

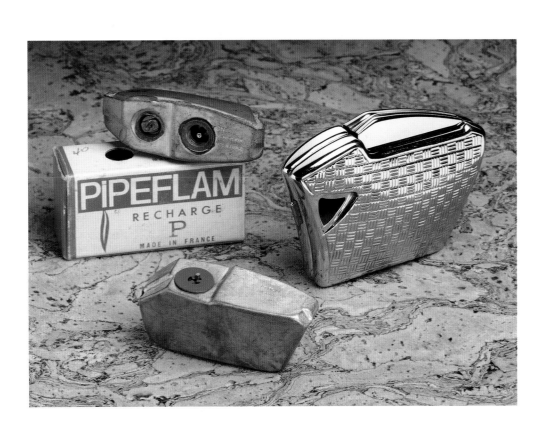

A: Beaufort gas and flint wheel pocket lighter by Flaminaire, France, 1959. Aluminum with chromium plating and plastic.

B: Flaminaire gas and flint wheel pocket lighter, France, c. 1960. Anodized aluminum.

C: Leader gas and flint wheel pocket lighter by Flaminaire, France, 1955. Brass with chromium plating.

Pipeflam gas and flint wheel pocket pipe lighter by Myon, France, c. 1955. Brass with chromium plating. Both a disposable and a refillable tank were made for this model.

·············

A: Star gas and flint wheel pocket lighter by Augusta, Germany, c. 1952. Brass with chromium plating and leather edging.
B: Augusta Zünder gas and flint wheel pocket lighter, model 200, Germany, c. 1953. Brass with chromium plating.
C: Super Fill gas and flint wheel pocket lighter by Consul, Germany, c. 1959. Brass with chromium plating. All three of these models were among the earliest lighters with detachable, refillable tanks.

respected lighter manufacturer Marcel Quercia, the son of legendary promoter of the Flamidor lighter, Janvier Quercia. Pingeot gave Marcel Quercia exclusive rights to produce the lighter, though the project was not immediately pursued, as industrial resources in France were quickly being directed to the war effort. Once the war was over, Quercia had little capital left, so he negotiated a deal with the large multinational Shell corporation to develop Pingeot's design for a gas lighter with a burner and filler valve. The Shell partnership was a great success and soon the Buta-bloc lighter was born, so named to identify the lighter's butane gas refill system.

Despite any postwar shortage of capital, Marcel Quercia remained on the forefront of innovation in the lighter industry. Quercia's ingenuity was widely applauded when he introduced a new gas lighter, the Flaminaire Gentry, at the Hotel Crillon in Paris in 1947. The success of this model inspired Quercia to perfect his design, and a year later he produced a pocket-sized Flaminaire lighter, appropriately named the Crillon.

Evidently, a new era was beginning in the lighter industry: manufacturers were starting to switch from gasoline to gas. The transition, however, did not promise to be easy. A gasoline lighter's primary component is the ignition device; in the gas lighter it is the burner and filler valve system. The mechanics of these parts needed to be technically refined; Quercia and other manufacturers had to further develop and perfect Pingeot's 1935 discovery that gas pressure in the lighter could be controlled by a valve, making it virtually independent of the pressure and temperature of the gas in the lighter's storage tank.

Converting gasoline lighters

A number of manufacturers were eager to produce gas lighters, but lacked the resources to create an entirely new product; instead, they began converting their existing gasoline-fueled models into butane gas lighters. At room temperature and atmospheric pressure, butane is gaseous (i.e., it vaporizes), but when kept under high pressure in a lighter tank, it stays liquid, and hence can be used and stored in much the same way as gasoline. These first butane gas lighter tanks adapted from the gasoline lighter models contained cotton wool to assist in the

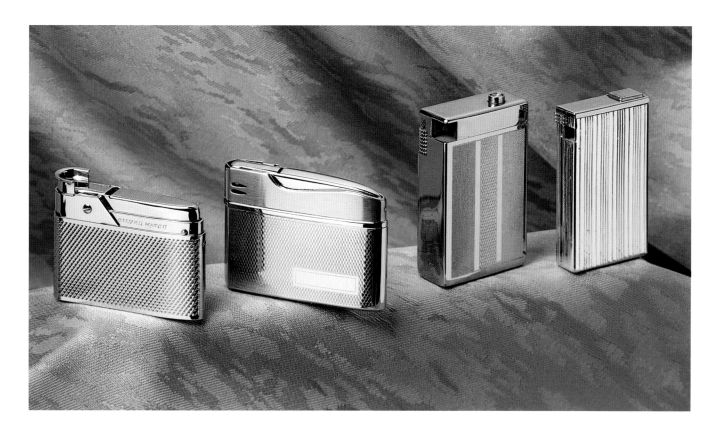

A: Compound gas and flint wheel pocket lighter by Silver Match, France, c. 1960. Brass with chromium plating.

B: Streamliner gas and flint wheel pocket lighter by Polly-Gaz, the Netherlands, c. 1968. Brass with chromium plating. Made by Sarome, Japan.

C: Gaz gas and flint wheel pocket lighter by Feudor, France, c. 1956. Brass with chromium plating.

D: Skyt-lady gas and flint wheel pocket lighter by Feudor, France, c. 1958. Aluminum. These three models all came with a detachable, non-refillable tank.

Right: Advertisement for Mylflam lighters.

Below: A: Vega gas and flint wheel pocket lighter by Feudor, France, c. 1955. Lacquered aluminum and brass with chromium plating.

B: Vega gas and flint wheel pocket lighter, model 13004, by Feudor, France, c. 1955. Lacquered aluminum and brass with chromium plating.

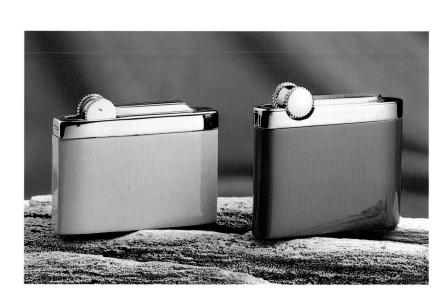

A: Piggy-Back gas and flint wheel pocket lighter by
Royal, Japan, c. 1965. Brass with chromium plating.
B: Bullet gas and flint wheel pocket lighter by Royal,
Japan, c. 1965. Brass with chromium plating; plastic
tank.
C: P.B.A. gas and flint wheel pocket lighter by
Sherwood, United States, c. 1955.
D: Stratoflame gas and flint wheel pocket lighter,
United States, c. 1955. Brass with chromium plating.

············

A: Tierce gas and flint wheel pocket lighter by Feudor,
France, c. 1967. Lacquered aluminum and brass with
gold plating.
B: Tropic gas and flint wheel pocket lighter by Feudor,
France, 1970. Plastic and brass with chromium
plating.
C: Gas and flint wheel pocket lighter by Poppell,
The Netherlands, c. 1960. Plastic and brass with
chromium plating. Poppell is among the relatively few
Dutch lighter trademarks.
D: Seven gas and flint wheel pocket lighter by Poppell,
the Netherlands, c. 1967. Plastic and brass with
chromium plating.

A: Special Femme gas and flint wheel pocket lighter by
Silver Match, France, c. 1965. Brass with gold plating
and leather .
B: Ultra Plat gas and flint wheel pocket lighter by
Silver Match, France, c. 1964. Brass with chromium
plating.
C: Dandy Classic gas and flint wheel pocket lighter by
Silver Match, France, c. 1967. Brass with chromium
plating and leather.
Silver Match launched all three of these appealing
designs within a short period of time. All of them came
with a detachable, non-refillable tank, and all were
made with interchangeable mechanisms – which made
them particularly popular among consumers.

• • • • • • • • • • •

conversion of liquid fuel into gas, a system that proved faulty
because the vapor phase burner valve was often blocked from
the cotton wool by wax. Foam replaced the cotton wool, but
soon it was evident that a liquid-only tank would work best.

The liquid gas tank required a special burner and filler
valve. One of the earliest and most successful designs for this
system was made by the Swiss company La Nationale, which had
been researching and creating lighter designs for various
companies since 1920. La Nationale produced burners and filler
valves for both Dunhill lighters and the Ronson Varaflame brand
that are still in use. Founded in 1905 by Richard Müller, Louis
Bourquin, and Fritz Montandon, La Nationale was privately
owned until 1985, when Conrad Zellweger, grandson of one of
the founders, sold the company to International Metals, a Dutch
firm located in Eindhoven, the Netherlands. Today, La Nationale
holds more than fifty patents for lighters.

Designs for the first gas lighters were relatively simple: a
lighting mechanism and a separate fuel tank enclosed in a
beautifully finished case. A dealer or manufacturer could replace
the fuel tank, although this was often both expensive and
complicated. The solution was a filler valve with a refill cylinder
and an improved, disposable tank that was the precursor of
today's disposable lighters. The technology for making filler
valves and burners improved along with further refinements to
fuel tanks, and eventually gas lighters with fixed tanks that could
be refilled with a cylinder (sold separately) were being made.

Improving the gasoline lighter

The development of gas lighters did not signal the end of the
gasoline-fueled models. Gasoline lighters continued to sell very
well, inspiring some manufacturers to look for ways to improve
their product. Theodor Ruetz, a dedicated Swiss inventor,
discovered a system that eliminated the need for a cotton wool
tank in the gasoline lighter – only a liquid gasoline tank was
needed.

Above: A: Feudor gas and flint wheel pocket lighter, France, c. 1960. Brass with gold plating and enamel.
B: France gas and flint wheel pocket lighter by Silver Match , France, c. 1961. Brass with silver plating and leather.
C: Myon gas and flint wheel pocket lighter, model 204, France, c. 1960. Brass with chromium plating.

Opposite: A: Arlac gas and flint wheel table lighter by Consul, Germany, c. 1963. Plastic and brass with gold plating.
B: Feudor gas and flint wheel table lighter, France, c. 1958. Brass with chromium plating.
C: President gas and flint wheel table lighter by Silver Match, France, c. 1962. Lacquered aluminum and brass with gold plating.
D: Gas and flint wheel table lighter, Germany, c. 1965. Bronze and brass; gold-plated handle.
E: Mylflam gas and flint wheel table lighter, model 320, Germany, c. 1960. Plastic and brass with chromium plating.

Silver-Match leaflets

Two demonstration models for the first filler valves developed by La Nationale of Switzerland. Both Ronson and Dunhill later based their filler valves on these early designs.

....

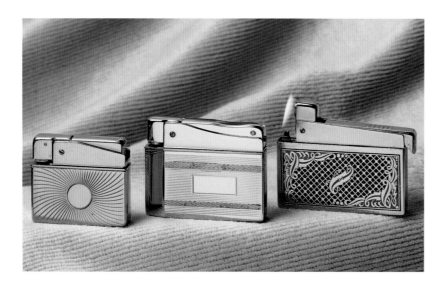

A: Gloric gasoline and flint wheel pocket lighter by Treibacher Chemische Werke, Austria, c. 1960. Brass with chromium plating.
B: Lord Carburator gasoline and flint wheel pocket lighter by Treibacher Chemische Werke, Austria, c. 1960. Brass with chromium and gold plating.
C: Classic gasoline and flint wheel pocket lighter by Karl Wieden, Germany, c. 1958. Brass with chromium plating and lacquer.
All three of these lighters operated on the Ruetz system, and were probably all made by Karl Wieden.

A: Tan-Anstalt gasoline and flint wheel pocket lighter, Switzerland, patented 1949. Brass with gold plating.
B: Tan-Anstalt gasoline and flint wheel pocket lighter, Switzerland, c. 1950. Brass with chromium plating.
Both lighters were designed according to the Ruetz system, and both were produced by La Nationale.
At left is the first Ruetz system design made with a ceramic burner; at right is a cross-section of a demonstration model made with a metal burner.

....

A: Ropp gasoline and flint wheel pocket lighter by La Nationale, c. 1952. Brass with gold plating. The original version of this lighter appeared on the market during the 1930s; it was updated with a Ruetz-system design, but this new model was never launched.

B: Liquid-I gasoline and flint wheel pocket lighter by Sarome, Japan, c. 1965. Brass with chromium plating. Like the Ruetz system lighters, this model contained no cotton wool in the tank.

C: Zündmetall Verkaufs Gesellschaft gasoline and flint wheel table lighter, Germany, c. 1962. Lacquered steel and brass.

D: Capri gasoline and flint wheel table lighter by Karl Wieden, Germany, c. 1958. Brass with chromium plating; silver-plated case.

• • • • • • • • • • •

(114): A: Two gasoline and flint wheel pocket lighters, Great Britain, c. 1946. Aluminum. The model to the left has two tanks and two flint wheels; the lighter on the right has one tank and two flint wheels.

B: Dub-l-ite gasoline and flint wheel pocket lighter by Beacon, United States, c. 1950. Aluminum. There are one flint wheel and two tanks on this model.

C: Twin Lite gasoline and flint wheel pocket lighter by Wifeu, Austria, c. 1950. Brass with chromium plating. This lighter has two tanks and an adjustable top.

• • • • • • • • • • •

A: Exalt gasoline and flint wheel pocket lighter,
Austria, c. 1930. Brass with chromium plating.
When this lighter was closed, a wick in the small tank
(built into the cover) pressed against the cotton wool in
the main tank, thereby refilling the small tank.

B: Twinlite gasoline and flint wheel pocket lighter by
Beney, Great Britain, c. 1948. Brass with chromium
plating. This lighter has a spare tank and wick in the
lift arm. When the lighter was closed, the tank was
refuelled via the spare wick in the main tank. When
the main wick was lit, the smaller wick in the lift arm
could be used to light a pipe.

············

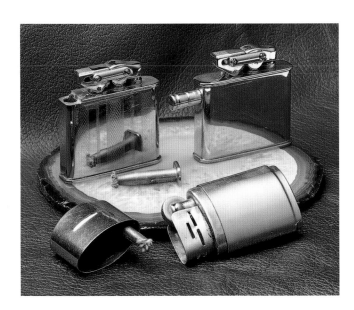

Ruetz collaborated on this project with La Nationale, and in May 1947 a patent for this system, called the Ruetz method, was submitted by a branch of La Nationale called the Tan-Anstalt company, located in nearby Lichtenstein. The Ruetz method involved a liquid gasoline tank that held a separate, sealed compartment, which acted as a cushion to absorb the differences in pressure created by the temperature change. The benefit of this technology was that the Ruetz tank held more gasoline; it needed to be refilled less often. Ruetz and Conrad Zellweger of La Nationale labored to perfect this new system, and they eventually produced and marketed the first Ruetz method lighter, the Tan Lighter. A few years later, the patent rights for the Ruetz method were sold to the Karl Wieden company, which launched a number of gasoline lighters using the Ruetz technology; other lighter companies soon followed KW's lead, employing a similar burner system in their new gasoline lighters.

Due to its continued popularity and to a number of technological improvements, the gasoline lighter maintained a position of market dominance until the late 1950s. A variety of different gasoline lighters were developed during the 1940s and 1950s that used a dual ignition system, such as the well-known duo/gasoline lighter, so named because it consisted of two lighters attached to each other, with two tanks, two wicks,

Gasoline and flint wheel table lighter, Great Britain, c. 1930. Brass with chromium plating. This lighter is similar in design to early models made by Colibri. It includes a spare wand, stored in a compartment behind the tank lid.

•••••••••••

A: Two Karl Wieden gasoline and flint wheel pocket lighters, Germany, c. 1935. Brass with chromium plating. These are both prototypes that never went into production.
B: Cyclone gasoline and flint wheel pocket pipe lighter, Great Britain, c. 1948. Brass with chromium plating.

•••••••••••

A: Jet-Stream gasoline and flint wheel pocket pipe lighter by Champ, Austria, c. 1950. Steel with chromium plating.
B: Lord Chesterfield gasoline and flint wheel pocket pipe lighter, Japan, c. 1955. Brass with chromium plating.
C: "JET", Britain, pat. 1929. Brass, silver plated.
D: The Beattie Jet Lighter gasoline and flint wheel pocket pipe lighter, United States, patented 1944. Brass with chromium plating and leather edging.

A: Sofabric gasoline and flint wheel pocket pipe lighter by Lanceflam, France, c. 1950. Aluminum.
B: Rocket Flame gasoline and flint wheel pocket pipe lighter by Rogers, Japan, c. 1958. Brass with chromium plating.

....

....

and two ignition devices. Variations on this included duo lighters with two ignition devices but a single tank and wick, and duo lighters with two tanks and a single, reversible ignition device. The advantage of the latter model was that when one tank was empty the ignition could simply be switched to the other tank.

Another "double system" lighter featured a separate tank with a wick mounted in the top of the cover. The lighter ignited when opened – the wick in the cover burned – and when closed, the wick remained contact with the tank and everything was concealed. This lighter became especially popular among pipe smokers, though it was not designed specifically for that market.

A gasoline lighter that produced two flames at once also found its niche among pipe smokers. The two flames were produced by two wicks, one in the main body of the lighter, one in the cover. Designed and sold in England by the Beney company, the "twin light" lighter is believed to have been the only one of its kind ever made.

Gasoline lighters made with a spare "match" – a metal wand – were also promoted as pipe lighters. The wand was held against the lighter's flame until it caught fire and then was used to light a pipe (or cigar, cigarette, etc.). The wand was then dropped back into gasoline tank, where it was once again immersed in fuel. This extremely popular model came in both table and pocket-sized versions.

Pipe smokers were also drawn to the remarkable jet stream lighter, an ingenious design that garnered a great deal of attention at mid-century. The first jet stream was patented on December 13, 1929 by Guy Strachan Barker of London, and two years later was marketed by John Beattie & Company in

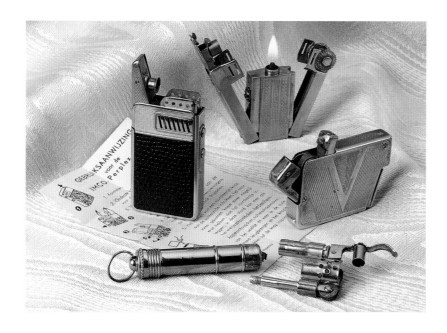

A: Firemaster gasoline and flint wheel pocket pipe lighter,
Austria, patented 1938. Brass with chromium plating and
plastic wheels. B: Perplex 6300 gasoline and flint wheel
pocket pipe lighter by IMCO, Austria, 1953. Steel with
chromium plating; leather shields. C: Record gasoline and
flint wheel pocket pipe lighter, Austria, c. 1920. Brass with
chromium plating.

············

England. An improved version of Strachan Barker's design was
patented in 1944 by Beattie Jet Products, Inc., based in New
York, and sold with great success in both Europe and the
United States. The jet stream lighter included a thin brass tube
that ran through a cotton wool tank; by slightly tilting the
lighter when ignited the flame heated this tube, which then
warmed the liquid gasoline in the tank, turning it into gas. The
increased pressure created by this reaction produced a spray of
flammable gas, creating a long flame that could easily light a
pipe.

Advertisement for Firemaster lighters.

············

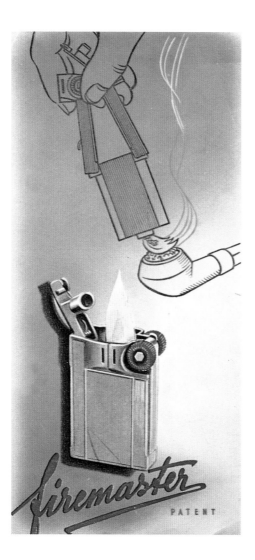

Pipe smoking: a unique ritual and an important market

The jet stream and various duo/gasoline lighters were perhaps
the first lighters that specifically addressed the pipe smoker's
needs. Since the early days of the lighter, manufacturers had
been trying to create models that would appeal to pipe
smokers; the short flame produced by the average lighter often
burned the smoker's fingers when lighting the pipe. Lighter
companies were anxious to remedy this problem and create an
efficient pipe lighter because of the considerable profit
potential associated with this market; pipe smokers have been
known for several centuries as a particularly enthusiastic and
loyal consumer group. "A happy smoker is no troublemaker,"
goes an old Dutch saying; lighter manufacturers have long
been eager to respond to the needs of this ideal, amiable client.

Since Ponce de Leon, Giovanni da Verrazano, and other
sixteenth-century explorers encountered Native Americans
smoking peace pipes in the New World, pipe smoking has
been associated with congeniality and contentment. The
explorers returned to Europe with countless intriguing and
mysterious tales about the tribesmen who stuffed dried
tobacco leaves into long pipes and inhaled the smoke as part of
a ritual celebrating pleasure and peace.

Pipe smoking was introduced in Europe by sailors who
discovered it was a good way to stave off hunger. Not
surprisingly, the earliest pipe-smoking centers in Europe were
bustling ports such as London, Bristol, and Hull, England, as
well as Hoorn, Enkhuizen, Amsterdam, and Den Briel in the
Netherlands. Soon, pipe smoking became popular among
Europe's upper classes, and by the end of the sixteenth century

A: Pipe-Mate gasoline and flint wheel pocket pipe lighter, Japan, c. 1965. Brass with gold plating and plastic edging.

B: Commander gasoline and flint wheel pocket pipe lighter by Nimrod, Great Britain, c. 1964. Brass and enamel.

C: Pipe Lighter gasoline and flint wheel pocket pipe lighter by Zippo, United States, 1984. Brass with chromium plating.

D: Windproof gasoline and flint wheel pocket pipe lighter by Zenith, Japan, c.1968. Brass with chromium plating.

E: Great gasoline and flint wheel pocket pipe lighter by Penguin, Japan, c. 1965. Brass with chromium plating.

F: Pipelite gasoline and flint wheel pocket pipe lighter by Polo, Japan, c. 1975. Steel with chromium plating.

G: Windproof gasoline and flint wheel pocket pipe lighter by Zenith, Japan, c. 1968. Brass with chromium plating.

This selection of pipe lighters are all based on the Zippo design. Nearly all manufacturers created their own version of the Zippo, either as gasoline or gas lighters.

pipe smoking had been elevated to a veritable cult; clubs were established that were dedicated exclusively to pipe smoking. Smoking became stylish among the well-to-do in England partly due to the efforts and antics of the legendary statesman Sir Walter Raleigh (1552–1618). Raleigh, who discovered and established the colony of Virginia, became a passionate smoker during his travels to the New World, and a number of anecdotes concerning his beloved habit persist to this day. One tale claims that the bold Raleigh bet Queen Elizabeth that he could estimate the weight of tobacco smoke. Before a court audience that included the Queen, he weighed the contents of a pipe bowl, then calmly smoked the pipe, tapped out the ashes and weighed them. The difference between these two weights – the pipe and the ash – was equal to the weight of the tobacco smoke, said Raleigh. Few spectators probably believed in the scientific accuracy of this performance, but many upper-class Englishmen did follow Sir Walter's lead and start smoking.

A: Touch-tip gasoline and flint wheel table pipe lighter by Ronson, United States, c. 1930. Lead alloy and bronze.

B: Pipette-T gasoline and flint wheel table pipe lighter by Prince, Japan, c. 1972. Plastic and brass with gold plating.

C: Royal gasoline and flint wheel pocket pipe lighter, possibly Japan, c. 1950. Anodized aluminum and brass with chromium plating.

D: Symbol gasoline and flint wheel pocket pipe lighter, Japan, c. 1952. Brass with chromium plating.

E: Super gasoline and flint wheel pocket pipe lighter by Baccy-Lite, Japan, c. 1955. Brass with chromium plating.

F: Golmet gasoline and flint wheel pocket pipe lighter by Benlow, Great Britain, c. 1950. Anodized aluminum.

G: Pipe gasoline and flint wheel pocket pipe lighter by Tommy, Britain, c. 1946. Brass, chromium plated.

H: Flambeau gasoline and flint wheel pocket pipe lighter by Flamidor, France, c. 1950. Aluminum.

I: Flambeau gasoline and flint wheel pocket pipe lighter by Flamidor, France, c. 1950. Aluminum.

J: Jhoro-Lite gasoline and flint wheel pocket pipe lighter, United States, c. 1945. Aluminum.

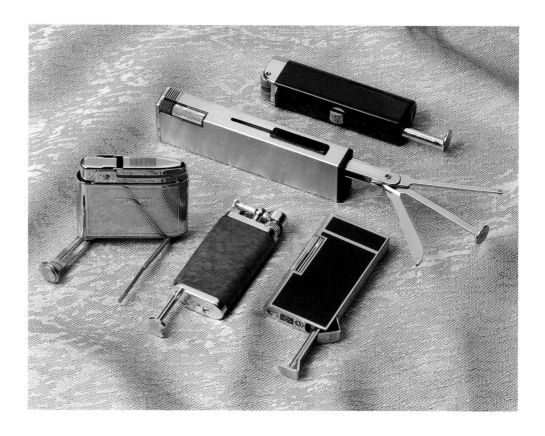

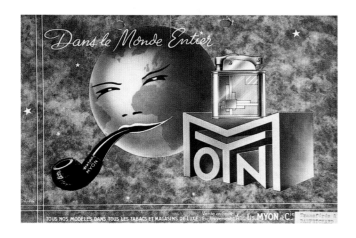

A: Feudor gas and flint wheel pocket pipe lighter, France, c. 1965. Lacquered aluminum and brass with chromium plating. B: Pipeboy gas and flint wheel table pipe lighter, Germany, c. 1974. Brass with chromium plating and plastic. C: Pipeservice gas and flint wheel pocket pipe lighter by Silver Match, France, c. 1966. Lacquered brass with chromium plating.
D: Old Boy gas and flint wheel pocket pipe lighter by Corona, Japan, c. 1985. Brass, silver-plated and briar case. E: Cavalier Pipe gas and flint wheel pocket pipe lighter by Zaima, Japan, c. 1973. Brass with gold plating and lacquer.

Brochure for a Myon lighter.

A: Pipe 18 gas with piezo ignition pocket pipe lighter by Corona, Japan, c. 1975. Brass with chromium plating and plastic.

B: Pipe Quartz gas with piezo ignition pocket pipe lighter by Marksman, Korea, c. 1981. Brass with chromium plating; plastic shield.

C: Bi-Jet gas and flint wheel pocket pipe lighter by Prince, Japan, c. 1968. Brass with gold plating. When the slide on this lighter was pushed forward, the flame moved to the front of the lighter and kept burning as long as the slide remained in this position, even when the top was released.

D: Jet-Lite gas and flint wheel pocket pipe lighter by Hilson, Japan, c. 1965. Brass with chromium plating.

E: Viking gas and flint wheel pocket pipe lighter by Ronson, Great Britain, patented 1952. Brass with chromium plating and anodized aluminum. The unique burner system on the Viking allowed it to be used as either a normal (cigarette) pocket lighter or — when the lighter was turned upside down and the resulting flame was lengthened — as a pipe lighter.

••••••••••••

A: Maruman gas and flint wheel pocket pipe lighter, model GL-67, Japan, c. 1970. Anodized brass.

B: Pipette gas and flint wheel pocket pipe lighter by Prince, Japan, c. 1970. Brass with gold plating and lacquer.

C: Flaminaire gas and flint wheel pocket pipe lighter, model 12, France, 1967. Brass with gold plating.
In this exceptional Flaminaire lighter, the burner opens and closes when the flint roller is turned on and off.

••••••••••••

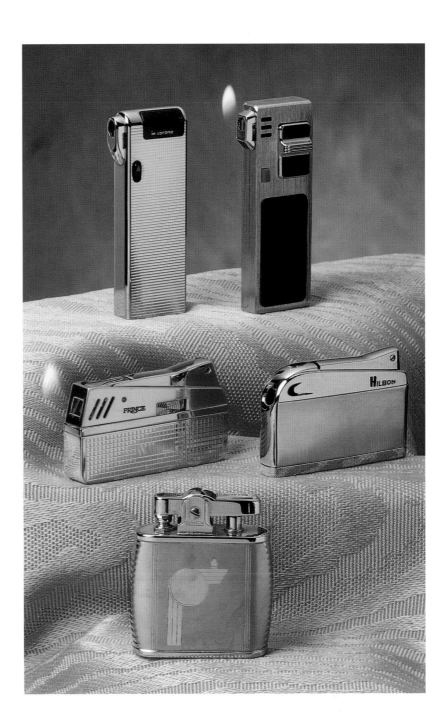

A: Filler gasoline counter refill can with pump by Thorens, Switzerland, c. 1950. Brass with chromium plating.
B: Gasoline counter refill can with pump, the Netherlands, c. 1950. Brass with chromium plating.

A: Verseur gasoline refill can by Flamidor, France, c. 1926. Lacquered steel with brass caps.
B: Flamidor gasoline refill can, France, c. 1930. Brass.

·············

Opposite: A: Gazobriquet lighter filling station, France, c. 1935. Brass with chromium plating.
B: Station Briquets lighter filling station by Pourrière, France, c. 1935. Bakelite, plastic, and brass.
C: Gasoline and flint wheel table lighter, Japan, c. 1955. In this model, the wand, which contains wick and cotton wool, is taken out of the side of the lighter and put in a hole near the flint wheel. Then it is ignited by operating the flint wheel.

·············

A: *Various disposable gasoline refill cans; a bag of flints; spare steel striker tips; spare flints for strike lighters.*

A: *Savinelli gasoline refill tube, Italy, c. 1962. Lacquered steel with brass cap.*
B: *Total gasoline refill cans marked "Rafinerie de Provence", France, 1959. Brass with chromium plating.*
C: *Junior gasoline refill tube by Shell, Great Britain, 1929. Lacquered steel with brass cap.*
············

Another famous myth about Raleigh maintains that he was swallowed by a crocodile during an expedition up the Orinoco River in South America. According to the story, the crocodile spared Raleigh's life and spit him out because he tasted of tobacco smoke. This tale spread quickly, and soon pipes were being made in the shape of a crocodile spitting out the explorer; these "Raleigh pipes" remained popular until the early eighteenth century.

Pipe smoking rapidly gave rise to a new industry: the manufacture of pipes and pipe accessories, all designed to enhance both the pleasure and the image of the pipe smoker. The first European pipes were most often made from clay pressed onto copper forms, copied from the original Native American design of a round bowl attached to a long stem through which the tobacco was smoked. Soon, pipe scratchers, tobacco jars and stoppers, as well as special racks and boxes for storing pipes began to appear on the market. The growing number of pipe smokers enthusiastically collected all the paraphernalia of their cherished habit.

Although the English certainly pioneered pipe smoking, historical evidence suggests that smokers in the Netherlands soon outnumbered those in the rest of Europe. One famous Dutch tale from the seventeenth century describes the frustration of a minister in Utrecht, who was so exasperated by his students' smoking that he angrily told them their "infernal fumes" reminded him of Sodom and Gomorrah's den of iniquity.

The world-renowned pipe-making industry that developed in Gouda, the Netherlands during the seventeenth century did owe much of its success to the early anti-smoking sentiments of the English king, James I (1566–1625). Unlike his predecessor, Queen Elizabeth, who herself had sampled a pipe thanks to Sir Walter Raleigh, James I had no tolerance for smoking. His fervent anti-tobacco policies drove a number of pipe makers to the province of Holland, and from there, to other parts of the Netherlands. No permit was required to start a pipe-making business in the Netherlands; all one needed was enough money to buy clay and a model form. Local potters were often called upon to finish the handiwork and embellish the pipes.

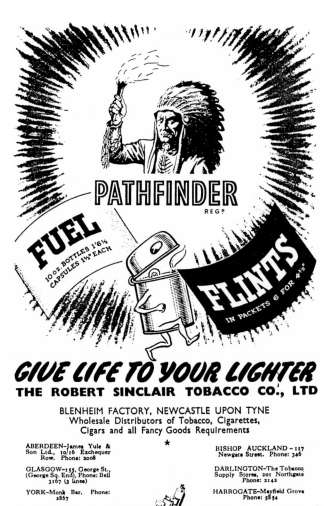

A range of disposable metal and plastic refill tubes. In the foreground is a tube with various refill nozzles and spare flints.

Advertisement for Pathfinder fuel and flints in "Tobacco" magazine.

The cities of Amsterdam and Gouda became the centers of the pipe trade in the Netherlands, though Gouda soon outpaced Amsterdam in production and was known for turning out the most beautiful pipes. Amsterdam remained important to the pipe industry because it was an important crossroad in most European trade routes. Gouda pipes were celebrated because of their unique designs and their larger bowl, which increased in size as the price of tobacco fell. Two Gouda designs were particularly popular: one had an image visibly carved onto the bowl, which became clearer as the tobacco was smoked and the clay was stained, and the other, known as the Churchwarden pipe, had a distinctive, long stem and was so fragile it had to be carefully preserved in a pipe rack when not in use. The golden age of the Churchwarden pipe was the eighteenth century; in 1749, the pipe makers' guild counted no fewer than 371 independent pipe makers in Gouda making Churchwardens for a variety of occasions and celebrations. In subsequent years, pipe makers continued to capitalize on the timeliness of certain images and designs, making special pipes to commemorate important dates and events.

The Dutch clay pipe was followed by pipes made from a variety of materials, including meerschaum (a light, clay-like mineral), porcelain, and wood. The meerschaum pipe was first introduced in Hungary and Austria, while the wood, or brier, pipe is said to have originated on the island of Corsica, where during the nineteenth century, devoted followers of Napoleon Bonaparte gathered annually to pay tribute to the late emperor's memory. According to legend, in 1855 a French pipe maker attending such a gathering broke his exquisite meerschaum pipe. An islander came to his aid and carved a new pipe for the Frenchman from the root of a brier shrub, something the Corsicans had been doing for years. The Frenchman proclaimed that tobacco tasted even better when smoked in the brier pipe than in the meerschaum, and decided to export brier to the village of Saint-Claude in Jura region of France. Within a year his commercial foresight paid off and Saint-Claude was home to a thriving brier pipe industry. The English were particularly taken with these wooden pipes; at the turn of the century, Alfred Dunhill claimed that ninety percent of all pipes made in Saint-Claude were exported to England. Variations on the original brier pipe include those

A range of early disposable gas refill tubes.

Disposable gas refill tubes with both pressure valve and screw-in valve.

••••••••••••

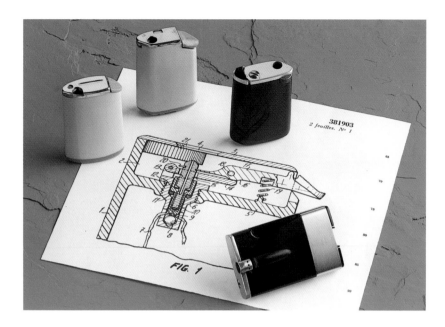

A: Prototype 1, Comet gas and flint wheel pocket lighter by Ronson, made by La Nationale, Switzerland, c. 1962. Plastic and brass with chromium plating. In this first prototype of the Comet, the entire top of the lighter had to be removed to change the flint; the flint wheel and gas control lever had to be operated manually.

B: Prototype 2, Comet gas and flint wheel pocket lighter by Ronson, made by La Nationale, Switzerland, c. 1962. Plastic and brass with chromium plating. The slide in the top of this model opened when the gas lever was moved to the left, thereby allowing easier access to the flint when it needed to be changed.

C: Prototype 3, Comet gas and flint wheel pocket lighter by Ronson, made by La Nationale, Switzerland, c. 1962. Plastic and aluminum with chromium plating. In the third version of this lighter, the entire top was designed to turn forward in order to change the flint.

D: Prototype 4, Comet gas and flint wheel pocket lighter by Ronson, made by La Nationale, Switzerland, c. 1962. Plastic and brass with chromium plating. This was the first fully automatic Comet prototype; unlike in the first three versions, the flint wheel and burner were no longer controlled manually. Also, the burner on this model is in the center of the lighter.

••••••••••••

A: Comet gas and flint wheel pocket lighter by Ronson, Great Britain, 1965. Plastic and brass with chromium plating. This was the first Comet design that went into production. The top of the lighter can be turned to change the flint, and there is storage space for one spare flint behind the flint wheel.

B: Comet gas and flint wheel pocket lighter by Ronson, model VC-10, Great Britain, 1967. Plastic and brass with chromium plating. This version of the Comet has a different transport mechanism than its predecessor, and there is storage space for two, rather than one, extra flints.

••••••••••••

A: Comet gas and flint wheel pocket lighter by Ronson, model 500-CW, France, 1968. Plastic and brass with chromium plating.
B: Two Comet gas and flint wheel pocket lighters by Ronson, model CW-22, Great Britain and France, 1967. Plastic and brass with chromium plating.

Ronson created numerous prototypes, as well as a variety of different models of the Comet; the company was striving, in part, to design a lighter that produced the exact proportion of gas and air needed in an efficient and reliable gas lighter.

A: Prototype of a Comet gas and flint wheel pocket lighter by Ronson, France, 1966. Plastic and brass with chromium plating.
B: Comet gas and flint wheel pocket lighter by Ronson, model SL, Mexico, c. 1970. Plastic and lacquered brass.
C: Comet gas and flint wheel pocket lighter by Ronson, model 500-SL, France, c. 1969. Brass with chromium plating.

Blason disposable lighter by Feudor, France, 1973. Perspex. This is a demonstration model.

....

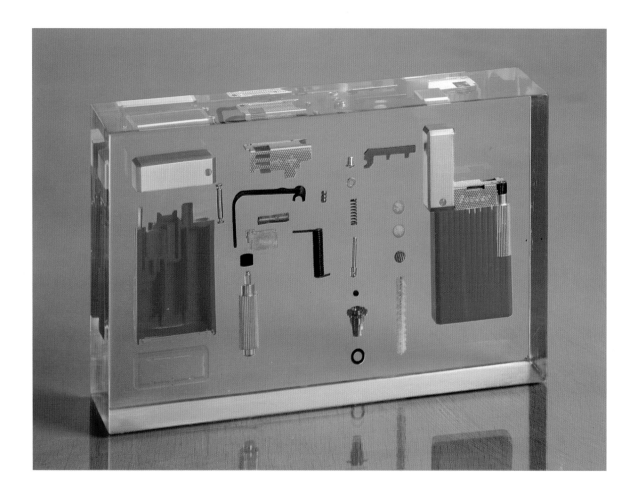

A: Stick gas and flint wheel disposable lighter by
Feudor, France, 1964. Plastic and gilded aluminum.
This was the first disposable lighter made with the
"la chute de pouce" (fall-of-the-thumb) system.
B: Cricket gas and flint wheel disposable lighter by
Samec/Dupont, France, 1962. Aluminum with gold
plating and lacquer. This was the first fully disposable
lighter ever marketed.

•••••••••••

made with mouthpieces of amber or vulcanized rubber.
Unlike cigars and cigarettes, pipes have always been valued as
both functional and decorative objects. Pipe smokers of the
last five centuries have cherished their pipes, preserving and
collecting them with enthusiasm. It is therefore not surprising
that lighter manufacturers have always been eager to
accomodate the pipe smoker's needs, developing specific
designs for pipes, and creating accessories such as pipe
scratchers and pipe stoppers built directly into the lighter's
base.

Lighter refills

The first "refill stations" for gasoline lighters appeared before
World War II, and operated in much the same fashion as
refueling stations for cars. From the 1920s on, tobacconists
refilled lighters by hand, charging a fee for each refill. They
also sold refill cylinders for use at home, so that there was
never a possibility that one might run out of lighter fuel.
Soon, there were also lighter refill stations that consisted of
gasoline dispensers hung on a wall or a counter in public
places, such as a cafes, restaurants, and tobacconists. Some of
these were automatic, dispensing the lighter fluid after a coin
was inserted in a slot. Gasoline dispensers gradually
disappeared during the 1950s, replaced by refill tubes.
Initially, the tubes had to be refilled, as they were expensive to
make, but later advances yielded cheaper models, and
eventually, disposable tubes. Plastic tubes, which held enough
gasoline for a single refill, were also made.The earliest butane
gas lighters also had to be refilled outside the home. At first,
the lighters had to be sent back to the factory to be refilled,
but later manufacturers appointed agents who could provide
this service to the company's clients closer to home. In order
to reassure customers of the agent's veracity and
qualifications, he had to be certified as a "recognized dealer"
by the lighter company he represented. Once gas lighter tanks
became safe and inexpensive to produce, disposable ones were
made and marketed under such names as Silver Match,
Poppell, and Feudor. And when a reliable refill valve was
developed for the gas lighter, refill tubes were also sold
independently, enabling customers to refuel their lighters
without the help of a lighter agent or tobacconist proprietor.

A variety of gas tanks from the earliest gas lighters.
Only the Olympic and the Consul are refillable.

A range of mechanisms made for early gas lighters.

The disposable lighter

The development of a completely disposable lighter was to have an enormous impact on Europe's lighter industry. By the 1950s, a very lucrative market existed for refill tubes and disposable tanks; many manufacturers were anxious to go one step further and make a fully disposable lighter, as the commercial potential of such a product was increasingly evident. By the end of the decade, the disposable lighter was becoming a reality. Once introduced, the disposable lighter was an overwhelming success; the design functions almost perfectly and the lighter requires no maintenance until the fuel tank is empty. This virtually flawless technology works by calculating, according to the tank capacity, the number of flames of a certain height and duration that the lighter can produce and the corresponding length of flint required.

This system was first seen by Marcel Quercia in the United States in 1953. The lighter was called the Flair, and a patent application for its design had already been submitted. The Flair worked on what later became known as la chute de pouce, or the fall-of-the-thumb system, in which the thumb rotates the flint wheel, and then drops onto the gas control lever, opening the burner. The remarkable thing about this operation is that the sparks that ignite the butane gas are produced before the burner valve is opened, so that the lighter essentially creates a flame with a single movement of the thumb. Innovative as it was in 1953, this system did not impress Marcel Quercia at the time; he did not foresee its impending proliferation and popularity.

In early 1961, a manufacturer named S.T. Dupont founded the Samec company in Paris with the idea of developing and launching a new, disposable lighter. Dupont hired Mouton de Villarep, who had worked for Marcel Quercia from 1949 to 1958, to run the firm, and on April 14, 1964, Samec introduced the first European disposable lighter, the Cricket. Extensive market research in France had shown that the name Façil was more popular, but the company settled on Cricket because of its more international sound. To make the Cricket, the Samec company had simply added a new flint device and valve to an earlier Dupont-designed gas refill. The only drawback to the Cricket was that it had to be closed after each use – otherwise, the unused gas would escape and create a serious fire hazard.

Shortly after the introduction of the first Cricket lighter, an inventor named Gilbertson developed and patented la chute de pouce system in France, and subsequently sold the patent rights to the Feudor company, a branch of Genoud & Cie. In 1964, Feudor launched the Stick, a disposable lighter that worked on this fall-of-the-thumb system. The Stick was immediately followed by a new Cricket, which also utilized la chute de pouce technology. Feudor, believing that the chute de

Four different Ronson service sets. These kits allowed owners to make basic repairs to their lighters without having employ the services of a dealer.

············

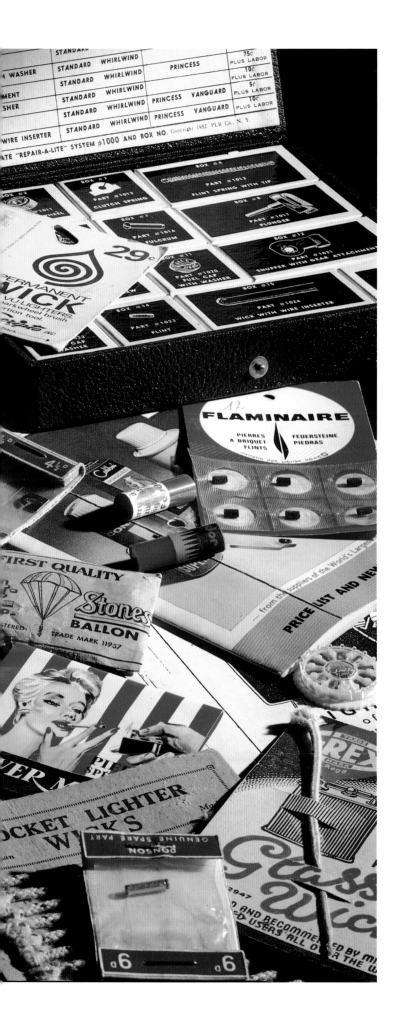

pouce system was protected by the Gilbertson patent, began legal proceedings against Samec. However, Mouton de Villarep remembered Marcel Quercia's discovery of the Flair lighter and its patent, and managed to trace the family of the original American inventor, who had since died. Family papers revealed that the Flair patent had never been honored, but because a patent can only be granted for a new, previously unpublished design, Gilbertson's patent was worthless. The case was dropped and Feudor and Samec settled privately.

The Comet

The widely successful Comet, produced and marketed by the Ronson company, was originally designed by La Nationale in Switzerland as a disposable lighter. Conrad Zellweger applied for a patent for this design in July 1962. Shortly thereafter, the Ronson company approached La Nationale about using the design for a plastic automatic lighter that had to be refillable and could be fully automatically assembled from the top. Louis Aronson II, grandson of Ronson's founder, was eager to make an inexpensive lighter that could compete with the new disposable models. The lighter had to be refillable, as Ronson did a flourishing business in refill tubes. The original design, along with these stipulations, was given to various factories in the United States, Britain, France, and Germany, each of which was asked to produce the Ronson Comet independently of each other. As a result, many different versions of the Comet were made and succesfully marketed in several countries at one time.

Turner's Box (left) and Ronson professional spare-parts set (right); Prince professional tool set (foreground, right). Manufacturers still provide sets like these to dealers and importers, though only for the more expensive models; most of the less expensive brands made today are not worth maintaining professionally.

A: A machine used to punch air holes in the burner caps of Ukay lighters, made in Great Britain. A Ukay lighter is in the foreground.
B: The Bedford gas with piezo ignition pocket lighter by Ukay, Great Britian, 1980. Plastic and brass with chromium plating. The lighter can be removed from its case when it needs to be refilled.

Production facility at Jbelo factory.

Service networks

Modern marketing techniques began to play an important role in the lighter industry after 1945. The service element of twentieth-century business practice was starting to flourish, and lighter manufacturers wanted to create as smooth and direct a path as possible to their customers. An entirely new branch of the industry sprang up as lighter producers attempted to better fulfill their clients' needs. Manufacturers began setting up service networks so that customers would know where to go for lighter repairs and spare parts. Dealers were appointed and given all manner of support in exchange for being contractually obligated to stock only certain lighter components. Like automobile companies and other successful businesses, lighter manufacturers also organized lighter repair classes and conventions for dealers where ideas and selling strategies could be shared.

Turner's Lighter Spares & Components of London was one of the first companies to capitalize on a perceived gap in the lighter service market. The Turner's Box, made from iron and filled with spare parts for various lighter brands, was sold to retailers and repair outlets with great success and remained popular for quite some time. Turner became a market leader, producing and stocking spares and components for every leading European brand of lighter.

Ronson followed suit with the Ronson Service Kit, a special repair box designed specifically for their customers' unique lighters. Before long, anyone who wanted to tinker with a lighter could buy a repair kit with the essential spare parts for his or her favorite brand.

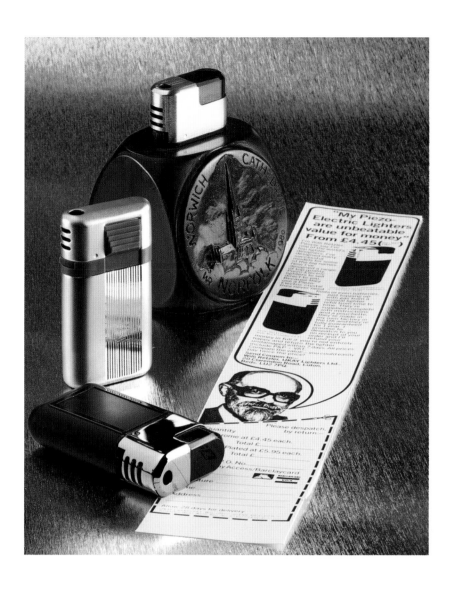

A: Ukay gas with piezo ignition table lighter, Great Britain, 1980. Limestone and plastic with gilded aluminum. This is one of a special edition of 800 hand made lighters.

B: Molectric 90 gas with piezo ignition pocket lighter by Colibri, Great Britain, 1978. Plastic and brass with chromium plating.

C: The Bedford gas with piezo ignition pocket lighter by Ukay, Great Britain, 1978. Plastic and brass with chromium plating.

Gasoline and flint wheel table lighter set, Japan,
c. 1955. Lacquered antimony with gold plating.

Willi Retzler

William "Willi" Retzler deserves special mention in the history of the lighter. Born in 1924 in Temeswar, Rumania, he emigrated to Britain in 1950, and in 1953 began working for Ronson as a designer. In 1962 he resigned as chief designer to take a break from what he was doing. Two years later he resumed work as a designer for a rival company, Colibri, and remained there until his retirement in 1982.

In the 1970s the Japanese lighter industry became competitive with European and American companies. Retzler decided to design a lighter that would be competitive, both in price and quality, with those being produced in Japan. With his employer's blessing he and his friend Ben Knight set up Ukay Lighters Ltd., in Luton, Bedfordshire, in March 1977. There he designed the Bedford lighter, which was available in four versions. Mike Peskin, who sold Japanese lighters in England under the Panther name, was so taken by the idea of an English lighter that he decided to also sell the Bedford under the Panther name. Retzler's boss, Jack Lowenthal, the son of Colibri's founder, included a modified version of this lighter, the Colibri Molectric 90, in the company's range. In 1980 a series of eight hundred handmade table versions were produced, but in 1993 the company was dissolved.

Lighter cases and sets

Until the 1950s, the value of a lighter was considered equal to the sum of its parts; up to that point, the various components of both gas and gasoline lighters were not truly autonomous. Once lighters were made with detachable tanks and other

141

Advertisement for Consul lighters.

Elegant gasoline and flint wheel table lighter set by Evans, United States, c. 1950. Steel, brass, and enamel.

....

Gasoline and flint wheel table lighter set, Japan, c. 1965. Antimony and silver plating; plastic butterfly.

disposable parts, however, non-technically inclined retailers could easily replace broken lighters. As a result, the lighter's case evolved into the most easily recognizable – and valued – component of the lighter. After the 1950s, more and more emphasis was placed on the design of the lighter case; it was the case that gave each lighter its unique identity and which eventually became synonymous with the lighter itself.

At mid-century, lighters were also increasingly being marketed as part of desks sets, in much the same way that they had been made and sold in combination with pens, watches, ashtrays, and clocks at the beginning of the century. Modern desk sets featured lighters in every conceivable design and were sold in every price bracket. A number of these were made from a metal alloy known as antimony, which became so popular in the trade that the director of a Japanese firm specializing in such sets was known in the industry as "Mr. Antimony." Today, lighter sets are made from a vast spectrum of materials, including onyx, silver, brass, aluminum, and plastic; sometimes the sets are covered with leather or inlaid with mother-of-pearl.

Pagoda gasoline and flint wheel table lighter set by
American Safety Razor Corporation, United States,
c. 1950. Plastic and brass with gilded aluminum.

Advertisement for A.S.R. Pagoda lighters.

Brilux gasoline and flint wheel table lighter set,
Switzerland, c. 1950. Brass with gold plating.

....

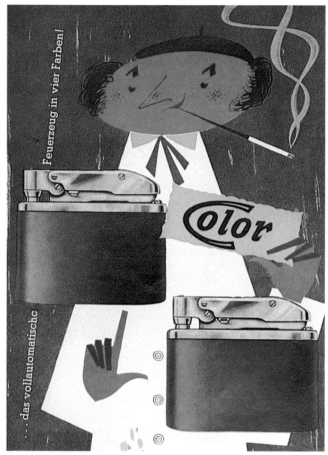

Advertisements for Consul Color and Transparento
lighters.

············

The growth of the Japanese lighter industry

The postwar industrial boom that invigorated the lighter and smoking markets in Europe and the United States also fostered the remarkable rise of the lighter industry in Japan. Before World War II, the Japanese had carefully monitored the development of the lighter industry in the West, copying European and American models to sell to the growing numbers of people who were taking up smoking in Asia. The smoking population in Japan and neighboring countries began to increase dramatically after the war, however, and Japanese manufacturers were zealously determined to capitalize on this expanding market. The Japanese had suffered defeat and widespread destruction, and they were intent upon regaining some of the pride and power lost on the battlefield by succeeding in the global marketplace.

As in Germany, the reconstruction of the economy in Japan owed a great deal to the aid and efforts of the United States, whose influence was felt worldwide after the Allied victory in 1945. American troops occupied Japan until April 1952; during the occupation a number of American lighter companies, such as Continental and Elgin America, set up offices and factories in Japan, profiting from a workforce that was both inexpensive and eager to learn. The Japanese also benefited from this arrangement, gaining knowledge and experience in the growing lighter trade. Between 1945 and 1952, all lighters produced in Japan carried the inscription "Made in occupied Japan." Today these lighters, like the

A: Zoom gasoline and flint wheel pocket lighter by New Light, Japan, c. 1959. Brass with chromium plating and leather.

B: Popo gasoline and flint wheel pocket lighter by New Light, Japan, c. 1959. Brass with chromium plating.

A: Gasoline and flint wheel table lighter, Japan, c. 1950. Ceramic and brass with chromium plating.

B: Lady Table gas and flint wheel table lighter, Japan, c. 1970. Ceramic and brass with chromium plating.

C: Bowler gasoline and flint wheel table lighter by Amico, Japan, 1962. Ceramic and brass with chromium plating. These three ceramic models are a small selection of the numerous lighters made to resemble figurines that have been produced in Japan.

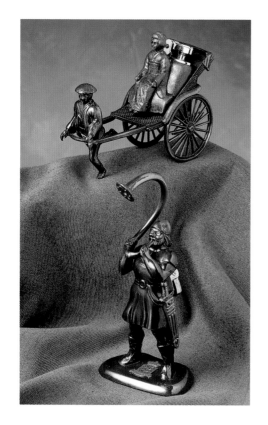

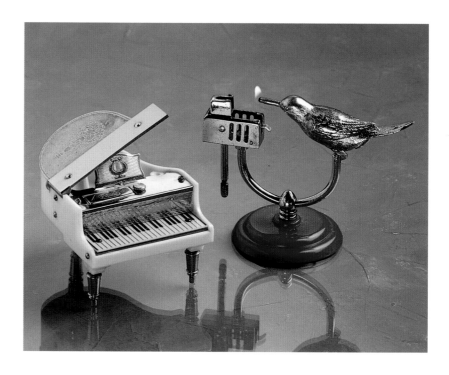

A: Piano gasoline and flint wheel table lighter by Prince, Occupied Japan, c. 1948. Bakelite and brass with chromium plating. Another version of this lighter was produced under the trademark "Clinton," and still another was designed in metal. All were made in occupied Japan shortly after World War II.
B: Tomo gasoline and flint wheel table lighter by Zaima, Japan, c. 1950. Antimony and brass with chromium plating and plastic foot.

Two gasoline and flint wheel table lighters, Japan, c. 1965. Antimony, brass, and bronze.

A: Compound gas and flint wheel pocket lighter by Silver Match, France, 1956. Brass with chromium plating.
B: Polly-I gas and flint wheel pocket lighter by Polly-Gaz, made by Sarome, Japan, c. 1961. Brass with silver plating and mother-of-pearl.
C: Powerflame gas and flint wheel pocket lighter by Polly-Gaz, made by Sarome, Japan, 1962. Brass with chromium plating and enamel.

············

trench-art and the early Zippo, are regarded as relics of an important era in recent history, and are highly prized by collectors.

During the 1950s and 1960s, the Japanese lighter trade began to flourish. Japanese lighter companies were starting to make a range of innovative and efficient lighters, both for domestic sale and for export to the United States and Europe. Some were copies of Western models, while others simply carried English names, such as Prince, Crown, Win, or Penguin. Before long, however, the Japanese lighter industry was establishing a powerful and distinctive identity on the international market. Soon, Japanese-made lighters were known for their fine craftsmanship and their ingenious, original design; Japanese lighters appeared in every conceivable shape and form, including animals, cars, boats, airplanes, radios, typewriters, cameras, beer and soda bottles, and small calculators and adding machines known as "ready reckoners." By the 1970s, the Japanese lighter industry was poised on the brink of global dominance.

Indeed, the Japanese economy not only experienced a phenomenal recovery, it was now beginning to challenge the leadership of the world's superpowers. During the early 1960s, in response to the growth of the Japanese lighter trade, the United States imposed a ban on the import of Japanese lighters. This was largely ineffective, however; the Japanese simply began exporting lighter components to the United States, where they were put together and sold. This venture was so successful that before long entire lighter sets were being shipped, assembled, and sold in the US.

Japan's nationwide zeal for economic strength gave birth to a lighter industry so efficient it also eventually threatened to wipe out its European competitors. Leading European designers and manufacturers attempted to meet this challenge by using the latest advances in plastics technology – more resistant materials, better mold designs, and the development of the ultrasonic welding process – to narrow the gap between inexpensive lighters and the more expensive engine-turned or diamond-cut finished models.

Three different models of the EMRO gasoline and flint wheel table lighter, the Netherlands, c. 1950. Brass with chromium plating and silver case; brass with chromium plating.

....

A: Barclay gasoline and flint wheel table lighter, Great Britain, c. 1948. Brass with chromium plating; anodized aluminum base.

B: Brown & Bigelow gas and flint wheel table lighter, United States, c. 1965. Brass with gold plating.

C: Kaschie gasoline and flint wheel table lighter, model K-35, Germany, c. 1950. Marked with a Lanvin of Paris trademark. Brass with chromium plating and enamel.

D: Bridge gasoline and flint wheel table lighter by Rowenta, Germany, c. 1956. Brass with chromium plating and mother-of-pearl.

E: Minton Pheasant gasoline and flint wheel table lighter, model RM-739, by Ronson, Great Britain, c. 1958. Brass with chromium plating and Minton bone china.

A: Standard gas and flint wheel pocket lighter by Mylflam, Germany, c. 1955. Brass with chromium plating and lacquer.

B: Rowenta gasoline and flint wheel pocket lighter, Germany, patented 1949. Brass with chromium plating and lacquer.

C: Lady gas and flint wheel pocket lighter by Heinrich Böhme, Germany, c. 1960. Brass with chromium plating and lacquer.

· · · · · · · · · · · ·

A: Prince gasoline and flint wheel pocket lighter, model R, Japan, 1961. Brass with chromium plating; plastic shield.

B: MG Auto 100 gas and flint wheel pocket lighter by Prince, Japan, 1965. Brass with chromium plating. The base on this lighter features a gauge that indicates when the lighter needs to be refilled.

C: Midget gasoline and flint wheel pocket lighter by Prince, Japan, 1959. Brass with gilded plastic shield. This tiny lighter could also be used as a tie pin or broach.

D: Prince gasoline and flint wheel pocket lighter, model JIS-2866, Japan, 1949. Brass with chromium plating and lacquer.

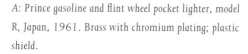

A: Golf Attache gas and flint wheel table lighter, model 12501-R, Germany, c. 1963. Brass with chromium plating and lacquer; plastic base.

B: Golf gas and flint wheel table lighter, model DC 9-T, by Golf, Germany, c. 1967. Brass with chromium plating and lacquer; plastic case.

·············

Pres-A-Lite battery/glowing filament car lighter and cigarette box by Masterbild Products, St. Louis, c. 1953. Bakelite and brass with chromium plating. This lighter was clipped onto the car's steering column and connected to the battery. The cigarettes were kept in a tray above the cigarette holder; a cigarette would be transferred to the holder when the lid on the tray was pulled down. The cigarette was then lit when it was pressed against the glowing filament.

·············

Advertisement featuring Bing Crosby.

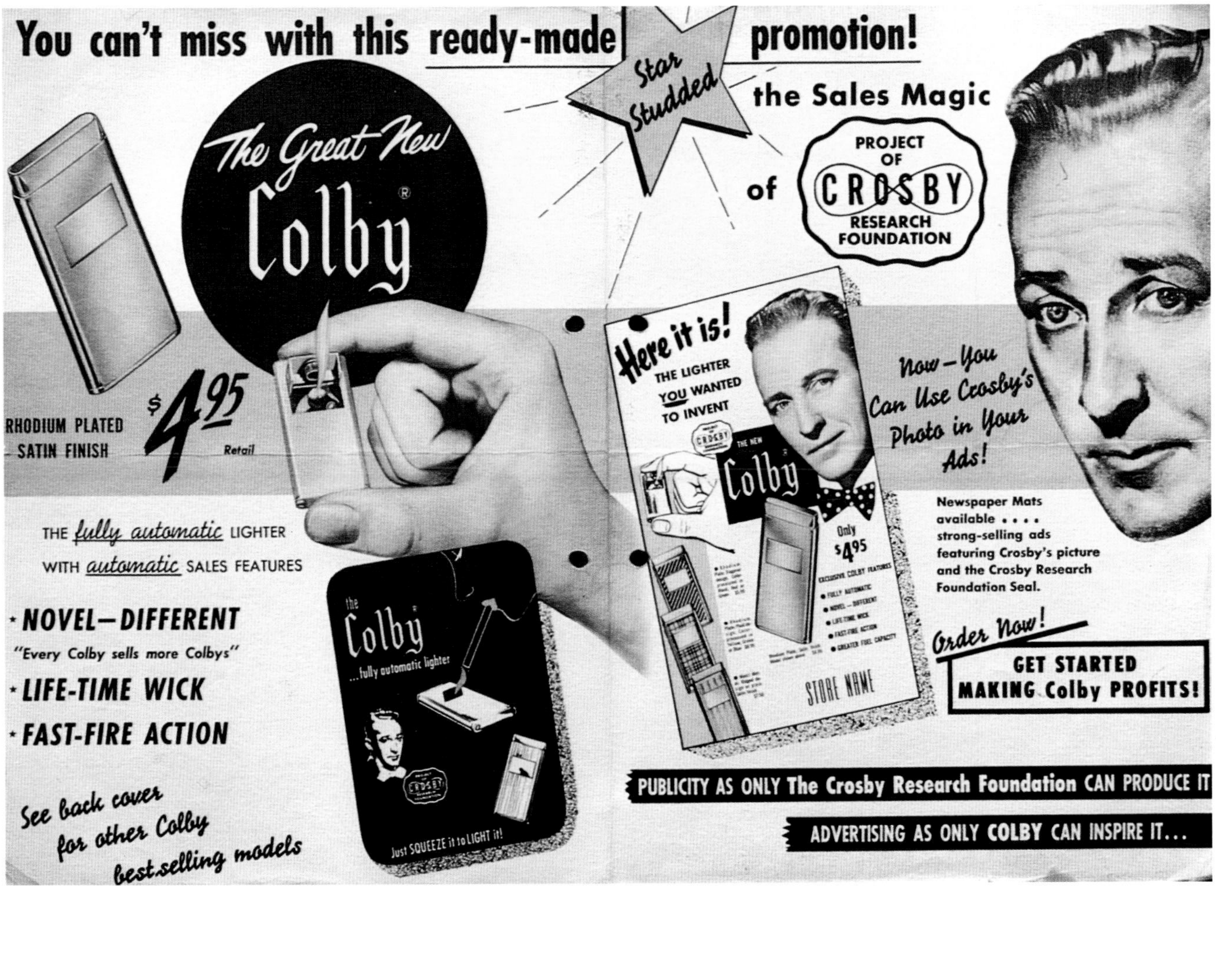

THE GLOBAL MARKET AND THE FUTURE OF THE LIGHTER

A New Era Dawns

The age of technology and mass marketing rose like a phoenix from the ashes of *World War II*, fostering tremendous advances and unprecedented levels of consumption in industrialized nations all over the world. By the early 1960s, consumers in Europe, Japan, and particularly the United States expected to reap the benefits of the latest technological discoveries.

A: Business gas with piezo ignition table lighter by Maruman, Japan, 1966. Brass and steel with chromium plating. This was the first lighter ever made with a piezo ignition, and it was designed in at least two versions. The first has a simple ceramic burner and a tank without a fuel gauge. The second has a dual ceramic burner/holder and a fuel gauge on one tank.
B: The piezo ignition mechanism for the Business lighter by Maruman, along with other piezo ignition designs.
C: Molectric 80 gas with piezo ignition pocket lighter by Colibri, Great Britain, 1967. Brass with chromium plating. This was Colibri's first piezo ignition lighter. A division of Colibri called Sapphire-Molectric applied for the patent for the lighter's piezo mechanism on February 27, 1963.
D: Rolls Royce Molectric 88 gas with piezo ignition pocket lighter by Colibri, Japan, c. 1969. Brass with chromium plating and enamel. This was a specially for Rolls Royce designed version of the Molectric made by Colibri.
E: Mercury gas with piezo ignition pocket lighter, model 7 DL-2/HIM, by Maruman, Japan, 1968. Brass with chromium plating. This was Maruman's first pocket piezo ignition lighter.

A: Varatronic gas with piezo ignition pocket lighter, model 3000, by Ronson, Germany, c.1975. Plastic. A cross-section of a demonstration model.
B: Varatronic gas with piezo ignition pocket lighter, model 1000 PX, by Ronson, Germany, c.1973. Brass and plastic. A cross-section of a demonstration model.

Electronic goods were now available to all, and people were eager to buy the latest appliances and gadgets, from refrigerators and televisions to stereos and lighters. Smoking was still immensely popular during the 1960s; the possibility that smoking was unhealthy had not been raised and the anti-smoking movement now prevalent in the United States had not yet mobilized.

The lighter industry was readily swept up into the tide of new technology and mass consumption; manufacturers strove to improve their products in order to meet the demands of their savvy customers. After the invention of the disposable lighter, producers began focusing their resources on developing new ignition devices for their lighters. The search for the ideal ignition device spawned a number of new lighter systems during the 1960s; it was an exciting and fruitful era for the lighter business.

Piezo lighters

The piezo ignition was one of the most important developments to emerge from this period of research and invention, although its origins date back to the late nineteenth century. The name piezo is derived from the Greek piezen, meaning "to press." In 1880, two French brothers named Pierre and Paul-Jacques Curie had discovered that when certain crystals are compressed in a particular direction, they produce electric charges. Under pressure, this piezo crystal produces a positive charge on one side and a negative charge on the other; under tension, these charges reverse. In order to maximize the amount of electricity, a hammer impact system is applied, which then produces a spark strong enough to ignite the gas in a lighter.

The first patent application for a piezo lighter was submitted in 1962 by Sapphire-Molectric, a subsidiary of Colibri; the designers responsible were Hans Lowenthal and Martin Paul Levey. Their invention was soon followed by a

A: Premier gas and flint wheel pocket lighter, model VF-604, by Ronson, Great Britain, c. 1964. Brass with chromium plating and leather edging.
B: Classic Novo gas and flint wheel pocket lighter by Karl Wieden, Germany, c. 1964. Brass with chromium plating; silver case.
C: Prototype of a Ronson piezo ignition lighter, Germany, c. 1970. Brass and steel. This lighter operates in much the same way as Ronson's Premier model.

D: Prototype of a Karl Wieden piezo ignition lighter, Germany, c. 1970. Brass and steel. This lighter is very similar to KW's Classic Nova. Both Ronson and Karl Wieden developed these prototypes simply by adding a piezo ignition to an existing model, thereby saving the expense of producing a completely new lighter.

·············

A: Maxim gas with piezo ignition pocket lighter, model 404 deluxe, Electronic, Japan, c. 1974. Brass with gold plating and lacquer. B: Molectric R-88 gas with piezo ignition pocket lighter by Colibri, Japan, 1974. Brass, enamel, and silver. This is another version of the Molectric 88. It was also produced in Japan by Crown under the trade name Mirage. C: Zaima gas with piezo ignition pocket lighter, model C-4, Japan, c. 1972. Brass with gold plating and lacquer.

·············

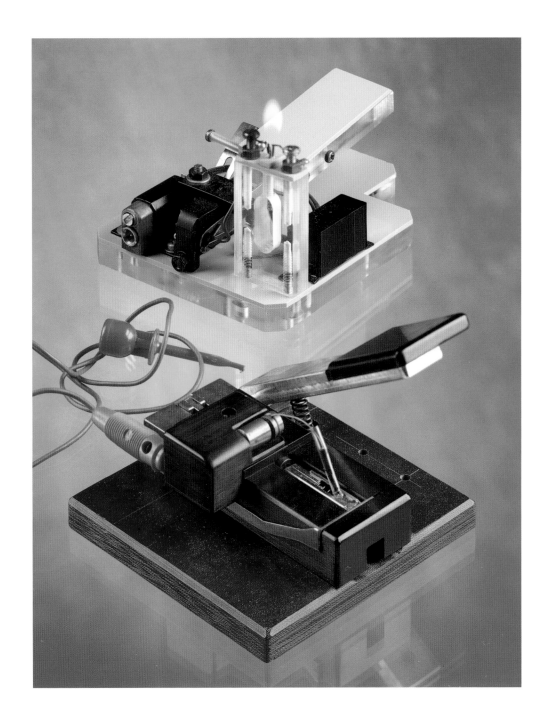

A: Prototype or demonstration model of a Ronson piezo
ignition lighter with a dual burner, Germany,
c. 1970. Plastic, brass, and steel. The two burners,
placed at different levels, were designed to ignite the
mixture of gas and air more effectively.
B: Ronson piezo ignition tester, Germany, c. 1970.
Plastic, brass, and aluminum. When connected to a
meter, this device reads the voltage of a piezo ignition.

············

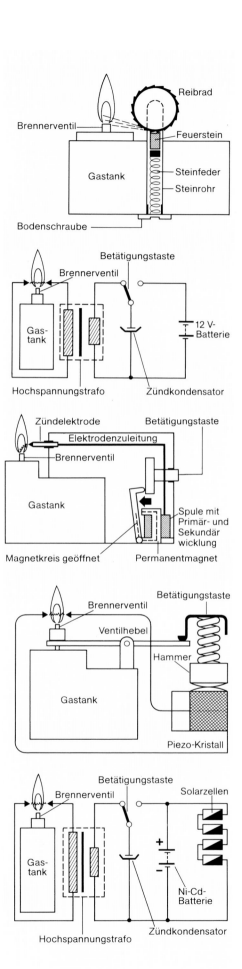

design for a Japanese piezo lighter, created by Mansei Koyo
Kabushiki Kaisa for the Maruman company. A patent
application for Kaisa's design was submitted in December
1964; working with characteristic Japanese speed and
determination, Maruman produced the first piezo lighter, a
table model called the Business lighter, just two years later. In
1967, Colibri introduced their version of a piezo lighter, the
Molectric 80 pocket-sized model.

The biggest glitch in the first piezo ignitions was that
their relatively small spark had to land in precisely the right
place in the stoichiometric mixture of gas and air in order to
ignite. Some manufacturers tried to solve this problem by
placing two burners of different heights next to each other, or
by using a double spark piezo ignition, as in the Tandem
model made by the Rowenta company. The innovative
Japanese finally came up with a viable solution by placing a
small, coiled spring around the burner nozzle, thus creating a
turbulent stoichiometric mixture around the spring; directing
the spark to the spring ensured a reliable ignition system.
Eventually, the piezo ignition became so refined that it was
used in disposable lighters.

Until 1970, Japanese lighter firms other than Maruman
had to pay royalties to Colibri for the use of the piezo patent.
The Japanese companies soon tired of this arrangement,
however, and took legal action against the British firm. Colibri

Rowenta ignition systems manual.

A: Beauton gas with piezo ignition table lighter by Bronica, Japan, c. 1969. Brass, plastic, and steel with chromium plating.
B: Esper-I gas with piezo ignition table lighter by Prince, Japan, c. 1968. Brass and steel with chromium plating and lacquer.
C: S-bird gas with piezo ignition table lighter by Prince, Japan, c. 1968. Brass and steel with chromium plating and lacquer plastic shields.
All three of these were among the first generation of piezo ignition lighters made.

....

lost the case, and the piezo patent was released, freeing the Japanese to perfect the piezo system in a variety of efficient and inexpensive lighters. A number of European companies attempted to develop equally reliable and affordable piezo ignitions, but they could not compete with the Japanese. Before long, many European manufacturers were simply importing piezo ignitions from Japan to put into their lighters.

Autoflint system

Ironically, Colibri's development of a piezo ignition undermined the success of another important discovery the company had recently made – the autoflint. Before the invention of this long flint, which was made to last up to a year, the spark system worked by the action of a spring pressing the flint against the flint wheel; only short flints could be used, and as these wore down the spring's pressure was no longer sufficient to generate the sparks necessary to ignite the lighter's wick or burner.

The autoflint system consisted of a flint tube long enough to house a twenty-five millimeter-long flint, which was pushed against the flint wheel by a small piston sliding within this tube. A concentric and outwardly sealed cylinder surrounded and communicated with this flint tube, and contained hydraulic fluid pressurized by a strong coil spring-acting on an annular piston. Because of the difference in volume of the cylinders, any displacement of the small piston caused by the

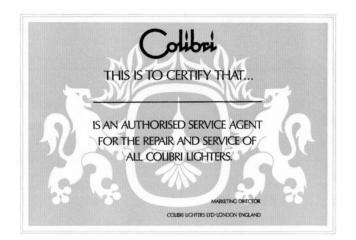

Certificate for Colibri service station.

Column gas and autoflint wheel table lighter by Colibri, Great Britain, c. 1968. Ceramic and brass with chromium plating.

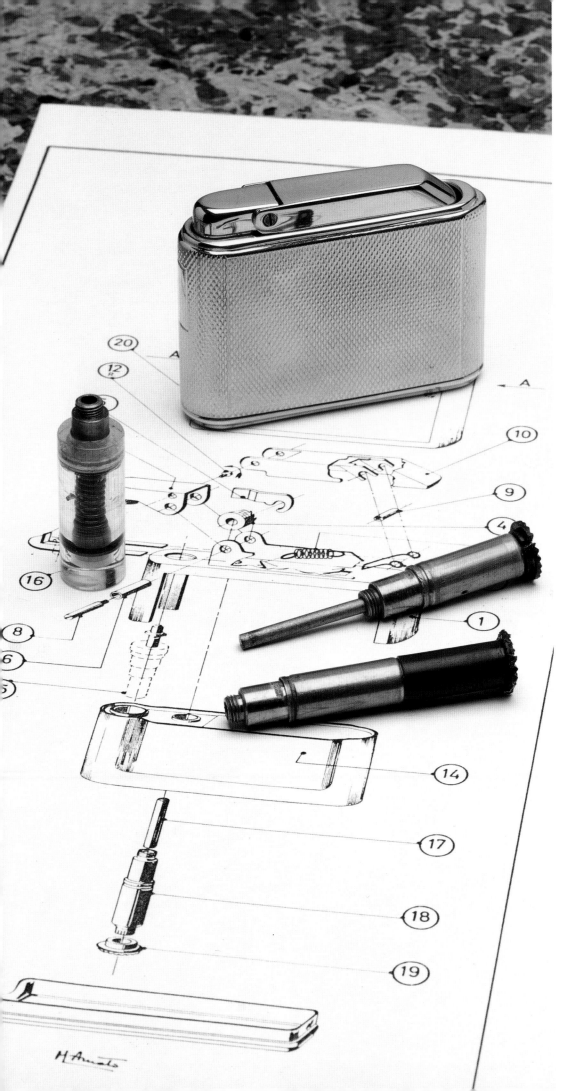

Colibri gas and Autoflint wheel pocket lighter, model H33-7901, Great Britain, 1968. Brass with 20 micron gold plating.

A: Cilindric T2 gas with electro-magnetic ignition
table lighter by Braun, Germany, c. 1968. Brass with
chromium plating and plastic .
B: F1 Mactron gas with electro-magnetic ignition
pocket lighter by Braun, 1971. Brass with chromium
plating; plastic shields.
C: TFG-1 Permanent gas with electro-magnetic
ignition table lighter by Braun, 1966. Brass with
chromium plating and plastic.

············

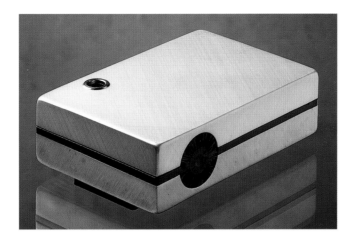

wearing down of the flint would hardly affect the piston in the large cylinder. The larger spring would not lose any strength or effectiveness, resulting in constant, effective pressure on the flint. Despite its success, the autoflint system achieved only a brief popularity, in part because it had to compete against the piezo ignition, which Colibri was actively researching and promoting.

Electromagnetic ignition

A particularly powerful new ignition system, the electro-magnetic ignition, was first conceived in 1911 when a Frenchman named Emile Laforge patented a magnetic spark ignition for lighters. No one expanded on Laforge's work, however, until 1960, when the Rowenta company applied for a patent for a butane gas lighter with a magnetic spark ignition. This electromagnetic ignition consisted of a powerful magnet enclosed by an iron core, which closed off the magnetic circuit, making it impenetrable except via a button or actuator. A coil was wound around part of the iron core, with one end attached to the burner and the other to an electrode nearby. By pressing a button the burner was opened and the magnetic circuit interrupted; the magnetic field in the coil was then altered, causing a spark to jump from the electrode to the burner. Later versions included a condenser in the circuit, which created a stronger spark and a more reliable ignition. The electromagnetic ignition system required no maintenance or replacement of batteries or flints, but it was relatively expensive and heavy. Nevertheless, other lighter companies, including KW and Braun, adapted the electromagnetic ignition system for use in some of their gas lighters.

Chemical ignition

During the first quarter of the century, when the lighter industry was first looking for alternatives to the flint system, some manufacturers researched an ignition based on a

Elomatic gas with electro-magnetic ignition table lighter by Karl Wieden, Germany, c. 1970. Brass with silver plating and plastic. The front foot acts as a sliding button to ignite the lighter.

Electronic 2000 gas with electro-magnetic ignition table lighter by Rowenta, Germany, 1966. Brass with gold plating and plastic and leather edging.

••••••••••••

chemical reaction similar to the reaction which takes place in lighters that use platinum as a catalyst in combination with methanol. This investigation continued through the 1950s, when the missile and aircraft industries also began experimenting with an ignition system based on a chemical reaction. In the United States, where a highly sophisticated space program was already taking shape, the Phillips Petroleum and Standard Oil companies were at the forefront of this pioneering research; in France, the Société d'Etude de la Propulsion par Réaction took the lead in investigating a chemical ignition system. The system involved adding chemical agents to butane gas, which created a spontaneous combustion when the mixture was exposed to oxygen.

Although this system posed obvious dangers for use in a lighter, an American company called Scripto patented a chemical ignition for lighters in 1964. The Battel Memorial Institute of Geneva developed a similar design. When Battel was sold in the early 1960s, its new owners were not interested in continuing this project, so the rights to the research were sold to LN Industries, which forged ahead with developing a chemical ignition lighter for Ronson. In August 1966, LN Industries patented the first prototype lighter with a chemical ignition. This chemical ignition system was first incorporated into a lighter made by the Ronson company in the 1960s, but like the electromagnetic ignition, this system had been the subject of considerable study years before. The system consisted of a sealed container filled with a chemical agent based on aluminum boron hydride; the container had a tiny hole at the top that was closed off with a pin, which acted as a valve. When force was applied to the actuator, the pin fell

A: Royal Musical gas and flint wheel pocket lighter with music box, Japan, c. 1964. Brass and anodized aluminum with gold plating. B: Supreme Musical gasoline and flint wheel pocket lighter with music box, Japan, c. 1960. Brass with gold plating. C: Flamsong gasoline and flint wheel pocket lighter with music box by La Nationale, Switzerland, c. 1955. Brass with gold plating.

•••••••••••

A: Muserock gasoline and flint wheel pocket lighter with music box by Prince, Japan, c. 1955. Brass with chromium plating. B: Muselite gasoline and flint wheel pocket lighter with music box by Prince, Japan, c. 1959. Brass with chromium plating and lacquer.

•••••••••••

A: Gasoline and flint wheel table lighter with music box, Japan, c. 1965. Brass with gold plating. The music box plays when the handle is lifted above the plate. The lighter is ignited by the revolutions on the switch.
B: Gasoline and flint wheel table lighter with music box, Japan, c. 1960. Plastic, brass, and steel with gold plating. The round button winds up the music box; both bobbins turn when the music box is played.
C: Eos gasoline and flint wheel table lighter with music box, Austria, c. 1955. Brass with chromium plating and leather edging. The lighter stands on top of the music box, which plays when it is lifted.
D: Schall gasoline and flint wheel table lighter with music box, Germany, c. 1957. Brass with chromium plating and leather edging. The music box is in the foot of the lighter; it plays when the lighter is lifted.

•••••••••••

Advertisement for Lancel in "L'illustration" magazine, November 15, 1930.

A: Eterna gasoline and flint wheel pocket lighter and watch, Switzerland, c. 1930. Silver and enamel.
B: Aircraft gasoline and flint wheel pocket lighter and watch, Great Britain, c. 1957. Brass with chromium plating.
C: Gisa Deluxe gasoline and flint wheel pocket lighter and watch, Switzerland, c. 1950. Brass with chromium plating and enamel.

············

A: Buler gas and flint wheel pocket lighter and watch, Switzerland, c. 1960. Brass with gold plating.
B: Buler gasoline and flint wheel pocket lighter and watch, Switzerland, c. 1950. Brass with chromium plating.
C: Gas and flint wheel pocket lighter and watch by Fero Feldmann, Switzerland, c. 1965. Brass with gold plating.

A: Time-L Cesar gas and flint wheel pocket lighter and LED watch by Crown, Japan, c. 1978. Brass and silver plating.
B: Time-L gas and flint wheel/battery spark pocket lighter and LCD watch by Crown, Japan, c. 1978. Brass with gold plating.

••••••••••••

slightly, so that a small amount of the chemical agent escaped and combusted on contact with air, lighting the butane gas. This prototype was actually similar designed as the Ronson's Comet lighter. The company director, Aronson, wanted to use this new chemical ignition system in a small lighter that included a pen, so the system was scaled down and refined as the Varachem, and incorporated into a model marketed as the Penliter. The Varachem system was also used in a standard pocket-sized lighter called the Sceptre; neither model stayed on the market for very long.

Improved battery lighters

Important advances in the electronics field, coupled with the widespread use of butane gas as lighter fuel, allowed for significant improvements to be made to battery-powered lighters. Developed at the end of the nineteenth century, the first battery lighters that used a glowing filament operated via a simple switch, which sent an electrical current through a high resistance wire, causing it to glow. The glowing filament was then used to directly light a cigarette or to light the fuel mixture – initially gasoline, and later, gas.

By the mid-twentieth century, with the use of butane gas and a greater understanding of how battery-powered electrical currents work, lighter manufacturers were able to develop an ignition system that used a battery-produced electrical current

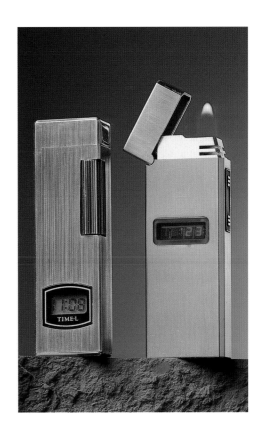

A: Pacton gasoline and flint wheel pocket lighter with pull-out tapemeasure, Japan, c. 1960. Brass with chromium plating.

B: Superior quality gasoline and flint wheel pocket lighter with pull-out tapemeasure by Crown, Japan, c. 1960. Brass with chromium plating.

C: Two gasoline and flint wheel pocket lighters with pull-out tapemeasure, Japan, c. 1955. Brass with chromium plating.

D: Measure II gasoline and flint wheel pocket lighter with pull-out tapemeasure by Atlas, Japan, c. 1965. Brass with chromium plating.

A: Glory gas and flint wheel pocket lighter and LCD watch, possibly Japan, c. 1980. Brass with gold plating.

B: Maxim gas and battery spark table lighter and quartz watch, model 4000, Japan, c. 1981. Brass with gold plating and enamel.

C: Kohgen II gas and flint wheel pocket lighter and watch, Japan, c. 1983. Brass with gold plating.

D: Montre Z-I gas and flint wheel pocket lighter and LCD watch by Maxim, Japan, c. 1984. Brass with gold plating and enamel.

·············

A: Pollyflame gas with piezo ignition lighter and watch, model EWL-8802, Taiwan, c. 1985. Plastic, aluminum, and stainless steel.

B: Romantic Watch gas with piezo ignition lighter and LCD watch, by Woodhouse, Japan, c. 1990. Plastic and aluminum with gold plating.

C: Jackflame gas with piezo ignition lighter and LCD watch and game by Monic/Miyamoto, Japan, 1982. Aluminum with gold plating and plastic.

············

to create a spark. This spark ignition system was far more efficient than the filament model, as it used far less energy to light the fuel mixture, and therefore required a smaller battery. Although a high voltage is usually needed to produce a spark – and lighter batteries normally produce currents no stronger than two volts – this system did not require particularly high voltage; a spark ignition can work with a high or low current.

The first spark ignition for a lighter consisted of a battery, a condenser, a coil, and a simple mechanical switch. The condenser acted like a buffer for the battery's current, while the coil provided the electrical charge. The switch determined the speed and strength of the spark's force. A microswitch was introduced in later models, which greatly improved the precision of this mechanism. The next refinement to the spark ignition was the use of a transistor, which can connect extremely quickly, creating a more powerful spark. The transistor connector was replaced when the Integrated Circuit (IC) system was discovered. The IC consists of several transistors connected together to produce a very fast, precise electrical connection. The IC eliminated the need for a "real switch," as the user triggers the IC directly, which connects the current and produces the spark. In addition, the IC has made the use of touch controls and light beams possible; a series of consecutive sparks can also be produced with the IC system.

Solar cell batteries

Another battery-powered ignition that was developed for lighters was the solar cell system, which produces electricity when exposed to the sun's rays. Depending upon the makeup of the solar cell, the electricity that is produced ranges between one-half and one volt – a very small charge. In order to increase the voltage, several cells are placed together in a series, but they still only generate enough of a current to slowly recharge a small battery. Once charged, the battery operates like any other, but its dependency on the strength of the existing sunlight makes this system relatively impractical. Only few solar cell battery lighters eventually appeared on the market; the best known are Rowenta's table lighters and the Prince pocket-sized lighter .

Gimmick lighters

Since the discovery of Auer metal at the turn of the century, lighter manufacturers have capitalized on current trends in design, fashion, and popular culture. Lighter companies and dealers have also assiduously promoted new developments in the manufacture of their products; any design that could be branded as "improved" or "amazing" has become important to a lighter's commercial success. Every era has seen its tastes – and its discoveries – reflected in the shapes, forms, and functions of the lighters made during that particular time.

RONSON
Varachem

Made in England

Varachem Cartridge Ignition

12
Ronson Varachem

Limited · Leatherhead · Surrey

Lighters that commemorate a specific event, person, or social convention have always been popular, as have lighters shaped like bullets, pistols, cars, and matchboxes, and those that include additional products or gimmicks – a small ashtray, pen, etc. Any feature or design that can be marketed as "different" or "new" has always been exploited by manufacturers and dealers eager to increase lighter sales. During the 1980s, for instance, a lucrative market for copies of old lighters developed, and countless variations of old-style lighters appeared.

In the age of mass marketing, lighters have provided an ideal venue for advertising logos, particularly for the trademark designs of cigarette brands. Lighters designed to illustrate or promote certain images or products proliferated with the advent of the disposable lighter, which made more expensive refillable models harder to sell. At first, the manufacture of so many different disposable lighters created an enormous waste of resources and energy; unfortunately, today, most disposable lighters cannot yet be recycled.

Relatively fewer types of lighters are being developed at the end of the twentieth century. Smoking has become less and less socially acceptable; the lighter is no longer the appealing gift it once was. Furthermore, safety standards for lighters have become more strict, especially in the United States, though European countries are expected to follow soon. New lighter designs may also have tapered off in the last two decades because the market was previously flooded with too many models.

A: Pocket lighter, Penliter AP228, gas with chemical cartridge and ballpoint pen, by Ronson, Great Britain, 1977. Brass with chromium plating.
B: Sceptre 55705, gas with chemical cartridge pocket lighter by Ronson, Great Britain, 1977. Brass with gold plating and enamel.
C: Sceptre 55703, gas with chemical cartridge pocket lighter, Great Britain, 1977. Brass with gold and chromium plating.

D: Prototype of a gas pocket lighter with chemical cartridge by La Nationale, Switzerland, 1968. Brass with gold and chromium plating. This was a prototype for both Ronson's Varachem Sceptre and Penliter models. It is marked "17B no.1 LN 12.86," and is clearly based on Ronson's Comet model, which was also designed by La Nationale. In the background is a box of spare cartridges; the cartridge in the foreground is a prototype.

A: Lasatron gas and battery spark pocket lighter by Colibri, Japan, c. 1982. Brass and silver. The Lasatron ignition is connected by an integrated circuit (IC) system and a light sensor. The IC is actuated by the interruption of a light beam.

B: Sensolite gas and battery spark pocket lighter by Tanita , Japan, 1975. Brass with chromium plating. This lighter is considered the first model to have a touch-tip switch – a combination of a microswitch and an touch-tip button.

Brochure for the Tanita Sensolite.

············

A: Vincy gas and battery spark table lighter by Flaminaire, France, c. 1973. Demonstration model. Plastic and brass with chromium plating. This model has a mechanical switch. The mercury ball in the lower glass part of the lighter ensures that the lighter can only be ignited when in an upright postion.

B: Electronic gas and battery spark table lighter by Rowenta, Germany, 1963. Brass with chromium plating. This model has a mechanical switch.

C: TE gas and battery spark table lighter by Sarome, Japan, c. 1977. Brass with gold plating; onyx shields. This model has a microswitch.

············

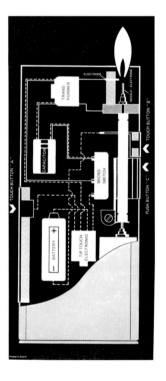

A: Marte II gas and battery spark pocket lighter with
microswitch by Bronica, Japan, c. 1977. Brass and
silver plating.
B: Excel gas and battery spark pocket lighter with
micro switch, model 141-S, by Prince, Japan,
c. 1971. Brass and silver plating.

···········

A: Jubileum gas and battery spark pocket lighter by
Maxim, Japan, c. 1979. Brass with gold plating and
enamel. This model has a repetitive IC connection with
touch button; when the top of the lighter is opened a
light in the touch button goes on.
B: Carven gas and battery spark pocket lighter, Japan,
c. 1981. Brass with gold plating and enamel. This
model has a repetitive IC connection, but the touch
button is made in the form of a flint wheel roller.
C: Calculighter gas and battery spark pocket lighter
with calculator by Satolex, Japan, c.1978. Aluminum
with gold plating. This model also has a repetitive IC
connection with touch button.

···········

A: Sunshine gas and battery spark/solar cell pocket
lighter by Prince, Japan, 1978. Brass with chromium
plating and enamel. This model has an IC touch-tip
repeater connection system with touch button.
B: Seurat glowing filament/solar cell pocket lighter by
Solar World, Japan, 1991. Plastic. In this model,
solar electricity is stored in a condenser. When the
lighter's slide is pushed to the "on" position, a current
runs through the glowing filament, generating enough
heat to light a cigarette.

···········

Opposite: A: Solartronic II gas and battery spark table
lighter by Rowenta, Germany, 1980. Brass with
chromium plating. This model includes a small,
rechargeable solar battery; the ignition is connected by
an IC and a push-button system.
B: Solartronic gas and battery spark table lighter by
Rowenta, Germany, 1973. Brass, plastic, and lacquer.
This is considered the first solar cell lighter. The solar
electricity is stored in a condenser, and the ignition is
connected via a microswitch.

···········

Electronic windproof lighters

One of the few new lighters developed fairly recently is the electronic windproof lighter. Research for the electronic windproof lighter appears to have begun in Austria during the early 1980s, but a patent for an Austrian electronic windproof design has never surfaced. The first patent for an electronic windproof lighter was submitted in Japan in 1986 by Seiko Kogyo, Ltd. Seiko Kogyo was founded in Tokyo in 1954 by Naraki Suzuki as a metal goods company. In 1977, the firm teamed up with New Light, Inc., to sell, distribute, and export its products. Seiko Kogyo was anxious to develop an electronic windproof design for gas lighters, which are notoriously sensitive to wind. The director of the company's research and development department, Yoshitsugu Naito, was asked to design a lighter that was not only windproof, but that also had a pure combustion system and was safe and easy to use. Initially, Naito's reseach department experimented with various different liquid lighter fuels, but these efforts proved unsatisfactory; the final version, designed in 1983 and patented three years later, called for an internal gas combustion system.

In the first Seiko Kogyo windproof lighter, the gas was pressurized by being routed through a miniscule hole while air was sucked in through small holes in the burner wall,

producing the correct mixture of gas and air. Via a distributor, this stoichiometric mixture reached a cylinder, where it was ignited by a spark from an electrode. The flame was protected in the cylinder by a piece of metal mesh with a catalytic filament, so that combustion occured entirely within the cylinder. According to this system, the catalyzer worked very effectively and the mesh screen became red-hot, guaranteeing a pure and safe combustion. This prototype was further refined in collaboration with Windmill Co., Ltd., and the final version was introduced on the Japanese market in 1986 as the Windmill Flameless 100. It was exported overseas a year later. Before long, other companies were granted manufacturing rights to the basic prototype and began producing their own versions of the windproof lighter.

Japan's organized lighter industry

Given the spirit of zeal and innovation with which the Japanese set out to conquer the lighter industry, it was not surprising that Japanese lighter manufacturers eventually formed an alliance to protect their interests. Ever since the postwar American occupation, the Japanese had directed considerable energy and resources to making and exporting mass-produced goods, especially small items such as watches, cameras, and lighters. The international market quickly bought up these reliable, streamlined, and inexpensive products, thereby spurring the phenomenal growth of Japanese industry.

The Japanese soon recognized that the export was vital to their economic success – the country is relatively small and has few natural resources. The foreign currency generated by the sale of goods in the global marketplace was necessary to keep the engines of Japanese industry running full-steam ahead. Japanese companies also realized that they could increase their strength on the international market by joining together to protect their trade interests. Japanese lighter manufacturers began to band together as soon as problems developed over the use of international patents, such as the struggle for the rights to the piezo ignition system that arose in the early 1970s. In 1976, the Japan Smoking Articles Corporated Association, an international lobbying organization for Japanese lighter manufacturers and dealers, was established under the direction of Michio Yosinaga, president of Yosinaga Prince Company. The association, which formed a partnership with the Japanese Chamber of Commerce and Promotion of Export (JETRO), initially included 130 lighter manufacturers and dealers – virtually all the Japanese lighter companies then in existence except Muraman. Today, JSACA membership has grown to 143, and its current director is Susuma Maruama, president of Windmill Co., Ltd. In addition to lobbying for trade rights and protecting Japanese patents, the organization publishes an annual sales catalog in both Japanese and European editions.

Nainen lighter

Just two years ago, the JSACA registered the name for a Japanese lighter that had been on the market for several years under various different trademarks. The Nainen, a name derived from the Japanese word meaning internal combustion, had been sold under several trademarks, including Flameless, Turbo, and Jetflame. In April 1993, Nainen became a registered JSACA name; association members now have exclusive rights to the Nainen internal combustion lighter, and the organization has applied for the name to be registered as theirs in South Korea, China, Hong Kong, and Britain.

Ikari lighter

In 1987, a similar lighter, called the Ikari, was patented in Switzerland by La Nationale. Like the Nainen, the Ikari used an injector and distributor to create an optimum mixture of gas and air, but the Ikari's cylinder was made from ceramic and had no metal mesh. The cylinder's special design created turbulence in the stoichiometric mixture so that combustion occured virtually within the cylinder. The Ikari system, unlike its Japanese counterpart, also used propane, rather than butane gas. Despite its unique, stylized design, the Ikari was never a success; it went out of production in 1991.

A: Oil-Well gas and battery/glowing filament table lighter by Zaima, Japan, c. 1971. Brass and plastic with gold plating. In this model, when the toggle switch is tilted forward and pressed inward, the gas lid opens and a filament next to the burner glows, thereby igniting the gas. A red light behind the toggle switch remains on until the switch is returned to its original position.
B: Baron gas and battery/glowing filament table lighter by Polly-Gaz, Japan, c. 1968. Brass with gold plating and leather.

....

A: Fumalux gas and battery/glowing filament pocket lighter with lamp, model FL 1000, Germany, c. 1963. Brass with chromium plating.
B: Gas and battery/glowing filament table lighter, Japan, c. 1970. Brass and plastic with chromium plating. The lighter's gas lid opens when a button is pressed on the small bar; as this makes contact with the female figure and the watering can, the filament next to the burner glows and ignites the gas.

A: Gloria gas and battery/glowing filament table lighter by Modern, Japan, c. 1965. Crystal, plastic, and brass with gold plating. This model is ignited by the white button. A lamp inside which turns red when the button is pressed, then blue, when it is released. When the button is pressed again, both the light and the lighter are switched off.

• • • • • • • • • • • •

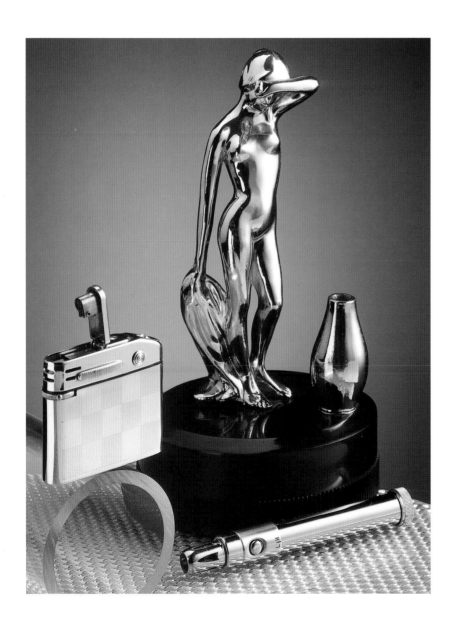

The collector's market

Although it is difficult to determine exactly when the lighter became the highly desirable collectible it is today, people have been buying and preserving unique models for many years. At the turn of the century, there was already a growing awareness of the social, historical, and cultural significance of the lighter. One important indication of this is that by about 1925, London's Briant & May Museum had amassed an impressive collection of various "fire-makers" that told the story of the lighter up to that time. Today the collection is part of the holdings of London's Science Museum.

The collector's market for lighters took off in earnest in the 1960s, when lighters of every description began appearing at flea markets all over Europe. At first, exceptional models could be bought for very little, but before long, lighters were all the rage, and were being sold in antique stores and other specialty shops. Prices rose considerably, as did the number of lighter collectors worldwide. Suddenly, there was a real need for organizations that could gather and distribute information for lighter enthusiasts. Clubs were formed in both the United States and Europe, but there was little international coordination between the various groups until the end of the 1980s, when the collector's market for lighters began to change dramatically.

In September 1987, the Dutch Lighter Museum Foundation was established in Eindhoven, the Netherlands. Dedicated to preserving the finest examples of lighters, and to gathering and disseminating all existing information in the field, this institution was the very first of its kind, and it has fulfilled a tremendous need. One of the museum's objectives is to make the vast amount of information on the lighter and its history available to anyone who is interested. A club of museum friends sponsors the Museum, which issues a special publication giving detailed information on all the lighters discussed in this book, and which publishes a quarterly lighter collector's journal exploring a variety of related topics.

Opposite: *A: Ice cream gas with piezo ignition pocket lighters by Monic, Japan, c. 1987. Plastic and brass. This is a typical display of Japanese novelty lighters. B: Golf Bag Clublite gas with piezo ignition pocket lighters, Korea, c. 1987. Plastic and brass.*

••••••••••••

A: Motor-Car gasoline and flint wheel novelty lighter by Lucky Car, Japan, c. 1950. Brass with chromium plating; plastic wheels. B: Jaguar 65 gasoline and flint wheel novelty lighter, Japan, c. 1965. Lacquered metal alloy and brass with chromium plating. C: Bug Street gas with piezo ignition novelty lighter by Beetland, Korea, c. 1986. Lacquered metal alloy and plastic. D: F-1 Car Lighter gas with piezo ignition novelty lighter by Pollyflame, Japan, 1988. Lacquered metal alloy and plastic.

A: Gasoline and flint wheel novelty lighter, possibly Japan, c. 1950. Lacquered metal alloy. B: Godzilla gas with piezo ignition novelty lighter by Beetland, Korea, 1989. Lacquered metal alloy. C: Popeye gas with piezo ignition novelty lighter, Japan, 1986. Lacquered metal alloy. D: L.N.Modern gas with piezo ignition novelty lighter, Japan, 1986. Lacquered metal alloy.

••••••••••••

A: Crystal Flash gas with piezo ignition novelty lighter with flashing lights by Marksman/Pollyflame made by Protime, Taiwan, 1989. Plastic and brass with chromium plating. When this lighter is ignited, light-emitting diodes (LEDs) flash on in random order; when it is ignited again, the LEDs go out. Designed by Richard Peersmann, this lighter sold 4.2 million copies in three years.

B: Guitarlighter gas with piezo ignition novelty lighter with electronic music mechanism and flashing lights by Pollyflame, made by Roburn, Taiwan, 1992. Plastic and brass with chromium plating. When the lighter is ignited, guitar music plays and LEDs flash on.

C: Sunset Flash gas with piezo ignition novelty lighter with flashing lights by Fun Flame, made by Protime, Taiwan. When the lid is opened, lights blink in both the case and the lid. Fun Flame is a registered trademark of Pollyflame.

D: Corner Flash gas with piezo ignition novelty lighter with flashing lights by Pollyflame, made by Protime, Taiwan, 1993. Plastic and brass with gold plating. When the lighter is ignited, a light in the base flashes red and green.

············

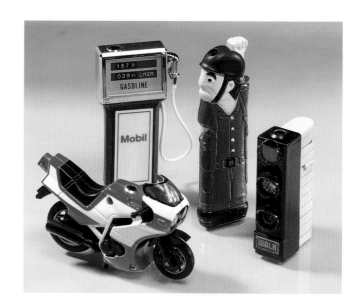

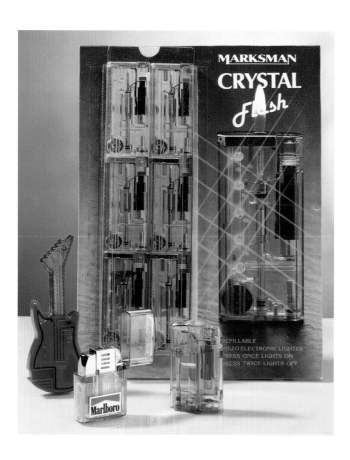

A: Gas Station gas with piezo ignition novelty lighter by Crown, Korea, 1989. Plastic and brass with chromium plating.

B: Soldier gas with piezo ignition novelty lighter, Japan, c.1986. Plastic and brass; lacquer helmet.

C: Trafficlighter gas with piezo ignition novelty lighter by Fun Flame, made by Protime, Taiwan, 1991. Lacquered plastic and brass. This lighter features flashing lights and a gambling game.

D: Bike Lighter gas with piezo ignition novelty lighter by Penguin, Japan, c. 1986. Lacquered metal alloy and plastic.

············

A display of novelty lighters.

············

A: O.E.M. gas with piezo ignition and Nainen burner
pocket lighter by Seiko Kogyo, Japan, 1986.
Demonstration model. Brass and metal alloy.
B: Flameless 100 gas with piezo ignition and Nainen
burner pocket lighter by Windmill, Japan, 1986.
Brass and metal alloy with gold plating and lacquer.
C: Flameless Pro gas with piezo ignition and Nainen
burner pocket lighter by Windmill, Japan, 1986.
Metal alloy and aluminum with chromium plating and
lacquer.

Ikari gas with piezo ignition and turbo burner pocket
lighter by La Nationale, Switzerland, 1988. Lacquered
brass and plastic.

• • • • • • • • • • • •

The Dutch Lighter Museum has not only become an encyclopedic resource center and a pivotal contact point for collectors and clubs from all over the globe, it has also fostered a marked growth of interest in the lighter. Since the museum's founding, prices at collectors' fairs and in antique shops have risen sharply, as has the number of books and articles written about the lighter's history.

Lighter collectors have increasingly begun to specialize in certain periods and types of lighters. Moreover, while collectors were at first primarily interested in gasoline lighters, gas lighters are now being eagerly bought up as well.

The collecting mania has not been lost on the lighter industry. As soon as a collector's market for their products existed, lighter manufacturers began producing special, whimsical models for collectors who wanted to add something distinctive to their collections. Lighter specialists now affirm that the pioneering days of lighter collecting are over; the lighter is an established, sought-after collectible, whose increasing number of fans will ensure the continued growth of this market. As a collectible, the lighter seems destined to amaze, amuse, and delight more and more enthusiasts.

The lighters of tomorrow

While the history of the lighter began in Europe, its future seems bound for Asia. Because Europe was home to most of the great scientific discoveries and advances of the eighteenth

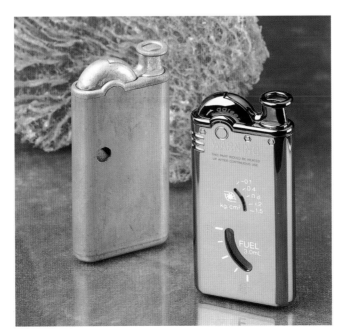

Brochure for Isaca Nainen burner.

A: *Agreer gas with piezo ignition and Nainen burner pocket lighter, Japan, 1988. Demonstration model. Brass and metal alloy.*
B: *AG 10 Turbin gas with piezo ignition and Nainen burner pocket lighter by Agreer, Japan, 1988. Anodized aluminum and lacquered metal alloy. This model features a gauge and a gas pressure meter.*

....

A: Convertible gas with piezo ignition and dual burner pocket lighter by Windmill, Japan, 1993. Brass with gold plating. There is both a normal and a Nainen burner in this lighter; the sliding button on the front allows the user to switch between them.

B: Maxim Bi-Flame US gas with piezo ignition and dual burner pocket lighter by Shanghai Double Flame Industrial Commercial Co., China, 1993. Brass with gold plating. In this model, the Nainen burner is activated when a button on the lighter is pressed in; when it is released the normal burner is in use.

C: Power Flame Plus gas with piezo ignition and dual burner pocket lighter by Colibri, Japan, 1993. Lacquered brass with gold plating. In this model, pressing on a button will first activate the Nainen burner, then the normal one; when the button is released, only the normal burner works. Jack Lowenthal of Colibri applied for a patent for this design on June 1, 1990.

A: Rotary gas with piezo ignition and Nainen burner pocket lighter by Maxim, made by Tae Woo, Korea, 1993. Brass and anodized metal alloy.

B: Madrid gas with piezo ignition and Nainen burner pocket lighter by Maxim, made by Hong Xing, China, 1994. Brass with chromium plating and lacquer.

C: Crown gas with piezo ignition and Nainen burner pocket lighter by Enzo Varini, made by Sales & Service, Korea, 1993. Lacquered metal alloy.

·············

and nineteenth centuries, the evolution of the lighter took place primarily in Austria, Germany, France, Britain and Switzerland. As the industrial revolution spread from these countries across the Atlantic, taking scores of skilled immigrant laborers to American shores, lighters were first mass-produced in Europe and the United States. The lighter industry reached its apex of production in the West shortly after World War II, however; the Japanese, who had eagerly copied the designs and practices of American and European companies, were soon poised to take over this lucrative market. By the 1960s, Japanese lighter manufacturers could take advantage of a thriving domestic market as well as an international demand for the efficient, inexpensive models their factories had begun turning out daily.

During the 1960s and 1970s, when a multitude of new, inventive lighters came on the market – improved battery and gas lighters, the piezo lighter – the Japanese established their leadership in the market by producing more innovative, reliable models in a more cost-effective manner than their Western competitors. Higher labor and development costs, coupled with a degree of market saturation, eventually drove a number of lighter factories in Europe and the United States to scale down or close altogether. The disposable lighter – which at one time was believed to threaten the survival of the match – buoyed up the Western lighter industry for a brief period, but before long the Japanese were making and exporting all lighters on a larger and more rapid scale. The lighter industry in Japan quickly expanded into neighboring countries, so that today, most lighters are made in Asia.

A: Dynasty gas with piezo ignition and Nainen burner pocket lighter by Maxim, made by Sunin Lee Master, Korea, 1992. Anodized and lacquered metal.
B: Compound gas with piezo ignition and Nainen burner pocket lighter by Spirit of Saint Louis, made by Hae Sung, Korea, 1993. Anodized aluminum and metal alloy with gold plating.
C: JY-L303 gas with piezo ignition and Nainen burner pocket lighter by Enzo Varini, made by Sales & Service, Korea, 1993. Lacquered metal alloy with gold plating.

Tokai gas with piezo ignition and turbo burner disposable lighter, model P-7, Japan, 1989. Plastic with aluminum shields.

A display of promotional lighters.

••••••••••

In the United States, the lighter industry has been especially hard-hit by the anti-smoking movement. Today, there are fewer American smokers than ever, and smoking is prohibited in more and more public places. And because of its association with smoking, the lighter is no longer a desirable gift in the United States. This trend seems to be slowly spreading to Europe, where a decreasing number of smokers will also undoubtedly yield poorer lighter sales.

Smoking remains immensely popular throughout Asia, however, and the high percentage of smokers in countries such as Japan, China, Korea, Taiwan are supporting a growing lighter industry. Moreover, Japan's traditional dominance is now being challenged by its neighbors, who are producing their own lighters. Taiwan and Korea, where low production and labor costs are the norm, appear to pose a particular threat to the Japanese.

China, which is home to over a billion of the earth's consumers, seems to be the promised land for the lighter industry of tomorrow. Not only is smoking exceptionally popular among the Chinese, the lighter is considered a status symbol and a distinctive gift in China. In recent years, most lighters sold in China were imported from Japan and Korea (a partial compensation for the Japanese and Korean companies' loss of revenue from declining European and American orders), but now the Chinese are entering the market themselves. At first, Chinese factories made only lighter components; today, there are a number of Chinese manufacturers producing their own brands of lighters. Huge quantities of lighters are streaming out of factories in Shanghai and Guangzhou every day. Mass-produced at minimal cost, these lighters are the lowest-priced the world has ever seen. Currently, they are being sold only on China's vast domestic market, but the day may soon arrive when the Chinese become the world's principal supplier of lighters.

A leap of centuries – and of the imagination – lies between the discovery of fire and the production of the modern, factory-made lighter. The fascinating evolution of lighter has been shaped by both inventiveness and idiosyncrasy, while scientific and technological progress have ensured continual advances in production methods, industry standards, and design. The lighter has kept pace with history, both embodying and reflecting the changes and challenges of each era. In essence, the lighter has always been a small but brightly burning beacon of progress, illuminating our path into the future. Looking at the tide of growth and innovation rising in Asia, it appears that the lighter's luminous mission is by no means complete.

DONORS

The following individuals and organizations have
donated lighters to the Dutch Lighter Museum
Foundation which appear in this book:

John Adler, Jerry and Annettta Agan, C. Ariës & Son,
Richard Ball, Jan van de Berge, Cris Bieshaar,
Juan Bochos, Lambert Bodar, Tom Clarke, Colibri,
Cremers Co., Ltd., Didier Dhaena, Ger van Doornink,
Isa van der Dungen, C. H. Genderen, Gerard Gerritsen,
Ton/Maik van der Geugten, George Gordon, Gubbels
Co., Ltd., Rob ter Haar, G.H. J. Hendrix/Bimalt Co., Ltd.,
Hirota & Co., Ltd., Frans van Honk, Kinzoku Kogyo
Ishimutsu Co., Ltd., Pierre Jaccard, Kawasaki Seiko Co,.
Ltd., Hermann van Keulen, Kogyo Koga Press Co., Ltd.,
Korea Crown, Jan van Lippen, Miyamoto
Manufacturing Co., Ltd., Rolf Muller, Tracy Musack,
New Light/Sayco Kogyo Co., Ltd., Guy Nishida,
Tom O'Key, José Onini, Wim Otten,
Richard Peersmann, Penguin Co., Ltd., Ira Philossof,
Pollyflame International Ltd., A. Prinsen,
Thomas Prylinsky, Willy Retzler, Boris and Maya
Rubin, van Slingerland Co., Ltd., Cor and Inge Snel,
Quina Span, Math Stultiens, Piet Suiker, Toshihiro
Okawa, N. Tsuchiya, H. Voll, Vribo Co., Ltd.,
J.A.C. Vrins, Yoshinaga Corporation,
Zaima Manufacturing Co., Ltd., Conrad Zellweger.

BIBLIOGRAPHY

Bidwell, Edward. *The History of Fire-Making.*
London: O. E. Janson & Son, 1912.

Bisconcini, Stefano. Lighters, *Accendini.*
Milan: Edizioni San Gottardo, 1983.

Brandes, Georg, and Rolf Jarschel. *Feuer und Flamme, Interesssantes vom Feuerzeug.*
Leipzig, Germany: VEB Fachbuchverlag, 1988.

Bucheit, Rita. *Geschichte der Feuerzeuge.*
Vienna: Christian Brandstätter, 1985.

Caspel, John. *Making Fire and Light.*
Woodbridge, Suffolk, Great Britain: Antique Collector's Club, 1987.

Christy, Miller. *The Bryant & May Museum of Fire-making Appliances.*
London: Bryant & May Ltd., 1926.

Cummings, Urban K. Ronson: *The World's Greatest Lighter.*
Palo Alto, Calif.: Bird Dog Books, 1992.

Dike, Catherine. *Cane Curiosa: From Gun to Gadget.*
Paris: Editions de l'Amateur, 1982.

Fresco-Corbu, Roger. *Vesta Boxes.*
Guildford, Surrey, Great Britain: Lutterworth Press, 1983.

Gouldsbloem, J. *Vuur en Beschaving.*
Amsterdam: Meulenhoff, 1992.

Heydenreich, Hasso. *Das Feuerzeug: Ein Beitrag zur Geschichter der Technik.*
Weimar: Weimar Stadtsmuseum, 1979.

Hough, Walter. *Fire-Making Apparatus in the US National Museum.*
United States: 1888.

Manchester, Herbert. *The Romance of the Match.*
New York: The Diamond Match Company, 1926.

Mercer, Henry C. *Light and Fire Making.*
Philadelphia: MacCalla & Company, 1898.

O'Dea, W. T. *Making Fire.*
London: Her Majesty's Stationery Office, 1964.

Pauschmann, J. A. Gottfried. *"Das Feuer und die Menschheit."*
Erlangen, Germany: Universität-Buchdruckerie, 1908.

Rushlight Club, The. *Early Lighting: A Pictorial Guide.*
United States: The Rushlight Club, 1979.

Scott, Amoret and Christopher. *Smoking Antiques.*
Great Britain: Shire Publications, 1981.

Seidel, Wolf-Dieter. *Vom Feuerschlagen zum Elektronikfeuerzeug:
Ein Beitrag zur Geschichte der Technik.*
Tübingen, Germany: Universitätstadt Tübingen, 1981.

Seyfried, Wolfgang. *Die Feuerzeuge: Vom Brennspiegel zum Solar-Zünder.*
Germany: 1992.

Tschudin, W. F. Sammlung Feuer und Licht. Olten, Switzerland:
Historisches Museum Olten, 1968.

Watson, Warren N. *Early Fire-Making Methods and Devices.*
Washington, D.C.: Gibson Brothers, Inc., 1939.

Wood, Neil S. *Collecting Cigarette Lighters: A Price Guide.*
Gas City, Ind.: L-W Book Sales & Publishing, 1994.

Page numbers in **bold italic** refer to illustrations.

Abdulla, **58**

A.D., **81**

Admira, **81**

Agreer, **181**; AG 10 Turbin, **181**

Aircraft, **164**

Airflam, **48**, 65

Altenpohl & Pilgram, **front cover**

Always, **60**

American Safety Razor: Pagoda, **143**

Amico, Bowler, **145**

A. P., **70**

Aronson, Louis, II, 137, 165

Aronson, Louis V., 57

Art Metal Works, 57

A.T.C., **19**

Atlas: Measure II, **167**

Atto, **65**

"Auermetall" lighter, **44**

Auer von Welsbach, Carl, 45-46

Augusta, **106**; Zünder, **106**

Auth, **56**

autoflint system, 158-61, **159**

Baccy-Lite, **121**

Barclay, **148**

Battel Memorial Institute, 163

battery lighters, 63-64, 165-67

Beacon: Dub-l-ite, **113**

Beattie, 118; Jet Lighter, **116**

Beetland: Bug Street, **177**; Godzilla, **177**

Begra, **65**

Beney, **76**, 89, 117; Twinlite, **114**; UL Popular, **92**

Benlow, 52, 89, **92**; Golmet, **97**, **120**; Three Wheel, **92**

Bernard, Jean, 89

Bewick &/Alese Bewick, **31**

Blaisdell, George Grant, 94

Bora, **75**

Bourquin, Louis, 109

Braun, 93, 161; Cilindric, **160**; Mactron, **160**; Permanent, **160**

Breveté, **59**

Briant & May Museum, 177

Brilux, **143**

Bronica: Beauton, **157**; Marte II, **171**

Brown & Bigelow, **72**, **148**

Bruma, **57**

Buler, **165**

Buta-bloc lighter type, 106

butane gas lighters, 104-9

Camlighter, **74**

Carven, **172**

Casco, **54**

Cauët, Luxuor, **71**

C.E.W., **49**

Champ: Jet-Stream, **116**

Champion, **81**

chemical ignition, 161-65

Christine Nilsson, **24**

Chronos, **79**

chuck-mucks, 19-20

cigarettes, 38, 154, 169, 185

CIVIC, 52

Clip-on, **85**

Clublite, Golf Bag, **176**

coal gas lighters, 73-75

Colby, **151**

Colibri, 52, **57**, **85**, 89, **115**, 141,
154, 156-61, **158**, **159**, 182; Autoflik, **92**; Column, **158**; Gaz-small, **103**; Lasatron, **170**; Molectric, 141, **153**, **154**, 156, **156**; Monopol, **103**; Power Flame Plus, **182**

collectors, 177-81

Consul, 73, **82**, **134**, 141; Arlac, **110**; Clip, **85**; Color, **144**; Super Fill, **106**; Transparento, **144**

Continental, 145

Corona, **18**; Old Boy, **122**; Pipe, **123**

Couic, **51**

Crown, **96**, 147; Gas Station, **178**; Mirage, **154**; Superior, **167**; Time-L Cesar, **165**

Custom, **20**

Cyclone, **74**, **115**

D'Alton Co.: Transfo, **60**

Dandy, **16**

Delite Superfine, **71**

Deniel's, **83**

Derby, **74**

desk sets, 142

disposable lighters, 135-37

Döbereiner lamp, 24, 27-29

double system lighters, 117-18

Drago, **99**

Dunhill, 89-91, 109; First Unique, **76**; Rollalite, **96**; Tusk, **74**

Dunhill, Alfred, 52, 89-91, 129

Dupont, **95**

Dupont, S. T., 135

Duralux, **54**

Dutch Lighter Museum Foundation, 177-81

Ebil, **93**

Eldred, **64**

Eldro, **70**

electric lighters, 59-63

Electrik, **77**

electromagnetic ignition, 161

Electronic: Maxim, **154**

electronic windproof lighters, 173

Eley, **90**

Elgin: Idalite, **85**; Light-o- matic Magic Action, **86**

Elsholz, Johann, 35

emery stone lighters, 32-33

Emil Deutsch, E.D., **79**

EMRO, **147**

Enzo Varini: Crown, **182**; JY- L303, **183**

Eos, **162**

E.P.H., **81**

Erlac, **80**

Eterna, **164**

Evans, **141**

Everest, **80**

Everflow, **71**

Ever Light, **82**

Evermatch, **68**

Ewiges Zündholtz, **47**

Exalt, **114**

Fabo, **66**

FC 555 Gun V, **18**

Fero Feldmann, **165**

Feudor, **41**, **74**, **95**, **110**, **111**, **122**, **133**, 135-37; Blason, **132**; Gaz, **107**; Skyt-lady, **107**; Stick, **133**, 135; Tierce, **109**; Tropic, **109**; Vega, **107**

Fire Chief, **47**

fire drills and bows, 15-16

Firemaster, **118**

fire piston lighters, 29-30

fire pots and horns, 15

fire steels, 16-18

Fischbach, Hans Wilhelm, **54**, 64

Flair, 135

Flamidor, 52; Duchess, **97**; Flambeau, **120**, **121**; Ouragan, 38; Verseur, **124**

Flaminaire, **123**; Beaufort, **105**; Crillon, 106; Galaxi, **102**; Galet, **102**; Gentry, **100**, 106; Grillon, **100**; Leader, **105**; Vincy, **170**

Franklin, **87**

Fulmen Pinel, **27**

Fumalux, **54**, **55**, 175; Dura-lux, **55**

Fumalux system, 64

Fun Flame: Sunset Flash, **178**; Trafficlighter, **178**

Fürstenberger, Johannes, 28

fusee lighters, 30-31

Garidon, **60**

gasoline lighters, 59, 106-17

Gazobriquet, **125**

G.D., **78**

Genoud & Cie., 135

Gilbertson (inventor), 135-37

Gisa Deluxe, **164**

Glamalita, **84**

Glory, **166**

Golf, **150**; Attache, **150**

Gorin, **25**

Guinn, **56**

Hadson, **85**, **86**

Hahway Company, **40**

Havalite, **84**

Heinrich Böhme: Lady, **149**

Helenix, **18**

Hera, **49**

Hilson: Jet-Lite, **123**

Hilton, **104**

Hinora, **60**

Homor: Elektro Lucifer, **50**

Ikari lighter type, 174, **180**

IMCO, 52; Föhn, **80**; Funkmeister, **66**; G11, **103**; Ifa, **80**; Jimco, **80**; Perplex 6300, **118**; Streamline, **16**; Super, **80**; Triplex, 52, **74**, **103**

International Metals, 109

Isaca Nainen, **181**

Ives, **11**, **32**

Jaguar 65, **177**

Jalumé, **52**

Japanese Chamber of Commerce and Promotion of Export, 174

Japanese lighter industry, 145- 47, 173-74, 183

Japan Smoking Articles Corporated Association, 174

JBELO, 52

J. Cassel, **22**

"JET," **116**

Jetflame lighter type, 174

jet stream lighter, 117-18

Jhoro-Lite, **121**

J.J.J. Carol, **85**

J. Meister & Co., 52

John Beattie & Company, 117-18

Jon Wonder Light, **40**

Kaori HI-Z, **69**

Karl Wieden, **44**, 52, **71**, **78**, **99**, **101**, **102**, 104, 115, **115**, **154**, 161; Capri, **113**; Classic, **112**; Classic Novo, **154**; Dorgento, **101**; Elomatic, **161**

Kaschie, 148

Kawasaki Seito, Esterd, **85**

Kimpel, **73**

Kiya, **53**

K. K. Apollo, **18**

Knight, Ben, 141

Knirps, **47**

Kohgen II, **166**

Köhlers, **28**

Köllisch Brothers, Consul Druco, **front cover**, **4**, **70**

Lady Table, **145**

Laforge, Emile, 161

La Metropole, **36**

La Nationale, 89-91, **96**, 109, **111**, **112**, 115, **130**, **131**, **132**, 137, **168**, 174, **180**; Flamsong, **163**; Ropp, **113**

Lanceflam, Sofabric, **117**

Lancel, 52, **164**

Lancel, Albert Alphonse, 52

Lanvin of Paris, **148**

Lektrolite, **49**; Glopoint, **50**

Lesansroulette, **60**

Levey, Martin Paul, 154

lighter refills, 133

lighters: brand names, 52-57; early, 24-33; future of, 181- 85; as gifts,

169, 185; gimmick and novelty, 167-69, 179; taxes on, 67-69

Light House, **77**

LN Industries, 163

L.N. Modern, **177**

L'Obelisque, **49**

Loewy, Raymond, 93-94

Lord, **83**

Lord Chesterfield, **116**

Lowenthal, Hans, 154

Lowenthal, Jack, 141, **182**

Lowenthal, Julius and Benno, 52

Lucifax, **40**

Lucky Car: Motor-Car, **177**

Lucky Strike cigarettes, 93-94

Ludwig Zwilling, **54**

Luminus, **25**

Lunström, Johan Edvard, 37

Luxuor, **74**, **75**

Lytic, **49**

Lytup, **92**

"Magic," **37**

Magic Case, **87**

Magic Introduction Co.: Koopman's Magic Pocket Lamp, **26**; Magic Wax, **30**

magic pocket lamps, 31

Magna, **54**

Mansei Koyo Kabushiki Kaisa, 156

Marksman: Pipe Quartz, **123**

Marksman/Pollyflame: Crystal Flash, **178**

Maruama, Susuma, 174

Maruman, **123**, **156**; Business, **152**, 156; Mercury, **152**; Thunder 7, **156**

Masterbild: Pres-A-Lite, **150**

matches, 35-38

Matchless, **32**

Matt Lighter, **91**

Maxim, **166**, **182**; Bi-Flame US, **182**;
Cliplite, **85**; Dynasty, **183**;
Jubileum, **172**; Madrid, **182**;
Montre Z-I, **166**

McMurdo, **83**

M.E.B., **78**

Mechaniece, **67**

methanol lighters, 65

Mico, **64**

Modern: Beretta, **16**; Gloria, **175**

Monic, **176**

Monic/Miyamoto: Jackflame, **166**

Montandon, Fritz, 109

Mosda, **57**

Mouton de Villarep, J. F., 135, 137

Müller, Richard, 109

Muraman, 174

Mylflam, **107**, **110**, **149**; Diplomat,
103

Myon, **111**, **122**; Pipeflam, **105**

Nainen lighter type, 174

Naito, Yoshitsugu, 173

Negbaur, **19**

netsukes, 20

New Device: Garidon, **60**

New Light, 173; Popo, **145**; Zoom,
145

New Yorker, **95**

Nimrod, Commander, **119**

Novitas, **51**

Nu-Line, **71**

Nuradon, **54**

Olympic, **134**

Omega Super, **61**

Oppenheimer Pipes Limited, 52

optical lighters, 20-21

Ora, Dicast, **93**

ORLIK, 52

Pacton, **167**

Pahaa, **97**

Palmer & Son, **35**

Panther, 141

Parker, **35**; Gondola, **47**

Pasch, Gustaf Erik, 37

Pathfinder, **128**

Pearl, **86**

Peersman, Richard, **178**

Penguin, **147**; Bike Lighter, **178**;
Great, **119**

Penlight batteries, **54**

Penlight batteries, **54**

Peskin, Mike, 141

Peyla, Louis, 35

Phillips, **74**

phosphorus matches, 35-37

piezo lighters, 154-58

Pingeot, Henri, 104-6

Pino, King, **76**

Pipeboy, **122**

Pipe-Mate, **119**

pipe smoking, 118-33

Pirona, **44**

Platina, **49**

Plenid, **67**

Pocketlamp: Reliable, **30**

Pollyflame, **166**; Corner Flash, **178**; F-
I Car Lighter, **177**; Guitarlighter,
178

Polly-Gaz: Baron, **174**; Polly-I, **146**;

Powerflame, **146**; Streamliner, **107**

Polo, 89, **92**; Pipelite, **119**

Popeye, **177**

Poppell, **109**, 133; Seven, **109**

Pourrière: Station Briquets, **125**

Premier, **57**

Prilinski, Thomas, 89, **90**

Prima Quality: Tresor, **73**

Prince, **136**, 147, **150**, 167; Bi- Jet,
123; "Clinton," **146**; Esper-I, **157**;
Excel, **171**; MG Auto, **150**; Midget,
150; Muselite, **163**; Muserock, **163**;
Piano, **146**; Pipette, **123**; Pipette-T,
120; S-bird, **157**; Straight-A, **69**;
Sunshine, **172**

Puck, **16**

P.X. Fox, **54**

Pyro, **90**

Pyrolux, **54**

Pyrus, **50**

Quercia, Janvier, 52, 106

Quercia, Marcel, 106, 135, 137

"Raketé," **60**

Rams, Dieter, 93

Ray-light, **20**

Ray-star, **21**

Razzia, **87**

Réchaud, 36

Record, **79**, 118

Reform, **86**

Reich, Otto, 104

repair kits, 138

Retzler, William, 141

Reutz method, 115

Ristex: Wrist-fix, **44**

Ritepoint, **69**

Rodenstock, 63

Rogers: Rocket Flame, **117**

Rolls Royce: Molectric, **152**

Ronson, 57, **135**, **137**, 138, 141, **154**,
155, 163; Banjo, **75**; Comet, **130**,
131, **132**, 137, 165; De-Light, **72**;
Minton Pheasant, **148**; Patrician,
86; Penciliter, **84**; Penliter, 165,
168; Premier, **154**; Sceptre, 165,
168; service kit, 138; Superpact,
86; Touch-tip (c. 1930), **120**;
Touch-Tip (c. 1938), **72**; Touch-
Tip Octette, **back cover**; Vanguard,
104; Varaflame, 109; Varatronic,
153; Verona, **104**; Viking, **123**;
Whirlwind, **104**

Rosedale, **93**

Rotral, **66**

Rowenta, **frontispiece**, **149**, **157**, 161,
167, **170**; Bridge, **148**; Electronic
2000, **161**; Solartronic, **173**;
Tandem, 156

Royal, **120**; Bullet, **108**; Musical, **163**;
Piggy-Back, **108**

Ruetz, Theodor, 109-15

Ruetz system, **112**

Rulag batteries, **54**, **55**

"Safety," **65**

safety matches, 37-38

Samec, 135-37

Samec/Dupont: Cricket, **133**, 135

Sapphire-Molectric, **154**

Sarasto, **44**

Sarome, **146**; Liquid-I, **113**; TE, **170**

Satolex: Calculighter, **172**